*An Education Track for Creativity and
Other Quality Thinking Processes*

"Once again your articles clearly outline every aspect of creativity for education, industry, and community as well as for government systems. More important, you have spelled out the importance of cooperation and integration that must be implemented within and among these organizations. To meet the increasing global competition that surrounds us, a country must seriously and clearly consider all the points you have indicated. Your messages are clear and concise. It must be done and it must be done now."

— Professor H. Norman Socha
Visiting Scholar, University of Cambridge
Scott Polar Research Institute, England

"In this work a passionate educator with 35 years of service from multiple educational perspectives speaks about her lifelong mission and the urgent goals that our educational system needs to address: the nurture of individual talents of students to maximize human resources for our global future; provide learning that is relevant, hands-on and intellectually stimulating; develop responsibility for preserving our natural environment; and, finally, the deliberately train for creative and critical thinking as well as for complex, systemic thinking. These are critical issues that today's educational institutions must take seriously if they want to prepare students appropriately for a complex, ever transforming, interconnected and interdependent future world."

— Cecilia Yau
Educational Consultant and Author, Education Foundation

"This collection of Bleedorn's insights and reflections on the quality of thinking are relevant for every educator and practitioner in every field of knowledge that exists in the world. I have spent over forty years as an educator, practitioner, administrator and consultant in health care. Not only is this book relevant in my field right now . . . but it is essential that we use this level of cognitive brain functioning in order to be responsible stewards of the future. Dr. Bleedorn's work is a clear guide for accomplishing the challenge."

— Dr. Marie Manthey
Founder and President Emeritus, Creative Health Care Management

"I am entirely in your corner with the concern for increasing creativity in schools and their ability to deliver quality thinking skills. Your writings provide a marvelous background for the creative thinking movement. As the British historian, who charted the rise and fall of civilizations, Arnold Toynbee, said, 'Those societies survive best that protect their creative minorities,' and 'where there is no challenge, there is no growth.'"

— Floyd Keller
Retired State Education Administrator

" 'You, there! What do you think?' This is the common question often posed by Dr. Berenice Bleedorn during a conversation or a presentation. She has been an excellent source and powerful force in the fields of creativity, quality thinking processes and futures studies for nearly forty years. These clearly written essays provide useful advice for and consultation with students, teachers and administrators in schools and among business leaders. I highly recommend these readings for those who seek to creatively transform good systems into better ones."

— Dr. Garnet Millar, Visiting Scholar
Torrance Center for Creative Studies
University of Georgia, Athens
Adjunct Professor, Department of Educational Psychology
University of Alberta, Edmonton, Canada

"In this new book Dr. Bleedorn has written a passionate argument for the evolution of our 'brain mind.' With uncommon exigency she demonstrates the interconnectedness and interrelatedness of our 'global village' and the absolute necessity for the explosion of higher orders of human thinking. She reminds us that each of us has inexhaustible creative energy which, as a catalyst for integrative thinking and learning, must be taught and incorporated into our educational system. It is imperative that, as our globe faces acute and challenging difficulties, Dr. Bleedorn's message be heard and heeded."

— Dr. Patience Dirkx
Research Psychologist
Editor of Bleedorn's previous book,
The Creativity Force in Education, Business, and Beyond

"This new book of Dr. Berenice Bleedorn is a cry! It is a loud cry for better education, for higher goals, for richer educational environment, for creativity in all educational areas, and especially for teaching the very basic processes for any life success: thinking! Never was there a better time for this book than now; it is right on target for the modern world. In addition to being of logical and methodological value, the book is written in a brilliant, language-rich but readable, complex, clear style. If I could use a citation for a final word, I would say, 'Two thumbs up!' "

— Andrei G. Aleinikov, Ph.D.
President, Montgomery Chapter, Phi Delta Kappa
International Association of Educators, President, Alabama Chapter
American Creativity Association, President, Mega-Innovative Mind International

An Education Track
for Creativity and Other
Quality Thinking Processes

Berenice Bleedorn

To Megan O'Hara
April 24, 2003
Many thanks for
your "creative advocacies"!
Bee Bleedorn

A ScarecrowEducation Book

The Scarecrow Press, Inc.

Lanham, Maryland, and Oxford

2003

A SCARECROWEDUCATION BOOK

Published in the United States of America
by Scarecrow Press, Inc.
A Member of the Rowman & Littlefield Publishing Group
4720 Boston Way, Lanham, Maryland 20706
www.scaroweducation.com

PO Box 317
Oxford
OX2 9RU, UK

British Library Cataloging in Publication Information Available

Library of Congress Cataloging-in-Publication Data

Bleedorn, Berenice D. Bahr.
    An education track for creativity and other quality thinking processes / Berenice Bleedorn.
        p. cm.
"A ScarecrowEducation book."
Includes bibliographical references and index.
    ISBN 0-8108-4550-4 (cloth : alk. paper) — ISBN 0-8108-4551-2 (pbk. : alk. paper)
    1. Creative thinking. 2. Thought and thinking—Study and teaching. 3. Educational change.   I. Title.
    LB1062 .B55 2003
    370.15'—dc21   2002010781

∞™ The paper used in this publication meets the minimum requirements of American National Standard for Information Sciences—Permanence of Paper for Printed Library Materials, ANSI/NISO Z39.48-1992.
Manufactured in the United States of America.

For all the creative, quality thinkers and activists who are working to make institutionalized education a place for practicing habits of thought that move society into newer, more just, and peaceful directions. You know who you are.

Contents

Foreword

HOW DO WE guarantee the right of every citizen to participate effectively in the task of building a more viable civilization? How do we develop students who can think critically, who can find creative solutions to the great world problems of our time?

Answers to these questions are the subject of Professor Berenice Bleedorn's new book: *An Education Track for Creativity and Other Quality Thinking Processes*. In this work, Professor Bleedorn demonstrates that if education is to prepare young people to function productively both at work and in society, it will have to introduce them to a wide range of tools including critical thinking procedures, creative problem-solving, conflict resolution, global and futuristic thinking, and systemic and paradoxical thought processes.

We have found that the world is not as ordered and predictable as we were led to believe for the past five hundred years or so. Not everything that is important can be apprehended by analytical thinking and logical thought processes. What we know and have been able to do so far is just a fraction of what we can know and do. At a time when familiar problems are no longer responding to established ways of thinking, and when new problems are defying conventional logic, Professor Bleedorn's new book presents the only feasible way forward.

This is not to deny the critical importance of logic, reason, and analytical thinking, especially when applied to appropriate sets of phenomena. But Professor Bleedorn is saying that these thinking tools, by themselves, are no longer sufficient to deal with the crises and uncertainties of our time. They cannot handle the higher level realities that are becoming increasingly central in our lives, nor can they produce the breakthroughs upon which further progress depends.

Professor Bleedorn provides us here with a blueprint for developing effective and deeply satisfied students. She gives us a method for ensuring the enhancement of their skills and self-confidence, a way of helping them to feel happy with themselves and with school.

I honestly do not see how any teacher, any educational policy maker, can be effective in this century without this book.

— Efiong Etuk, Ph.D.
Senior Scholar, Unity Scholars
Author of *Great Insights on Human Creativity:
Transforming the Way We Live,
Work, Educate, Lead, and Relate*

Light at the End of the Tunnel

THERE ARE DEFINITE signs of a global crisis in education because the "sell-by date" of the present education system has long since expired. Public education as we know it today is a product of the Industrial Revolution. In spite of the fact that the world has changed dramatically, the aim and the ethos of the education system are in many ways exactly the same as 300 years ago: to send children to school for twelve years in order to produce people capable of working for someone else without asking too many questions. In many parts of the world this goal is still reinforced by the wearing of formal school uniforms and a disciplinary system that puts the emphasis on regimentation instead of on self-discipline.

Before the Industrial Revolution, the state played no role in public education. It was mainly in the hands of the church and independent guilds. The church taught people to read and write with academic and church-oriented careers in mind. The guilds in turn provided apprenticeships in a particular trade, which would enable one to successfully establish a business of one's own.

The Industrial Revolution put an end to the guilds and their independent tradespeople. It resulted in thousands of unemployed flocking to the cities seeking jobs as laborers in the new factories. Men and women worked to sustain their families, resulting in latchkey children roaming the cities. To combat the associated social evils the state turned to the educational arena. But it did not forget the needs of the factory bosses who paid the taxes. The objective of this new kind of education was not to deliver people capable of providing for themselves, but laborers conditioned to do boring and repetitive work for someone else without questioning "the system."

Creativity was not expected of them. Because only one "correct" system allowed a factory to function efficiently, the school system adapted itself to this idea. Whereas the guild system emphasized self-reliance and self-discipline, the emphasis now shifted to regimentation. Learners were thought of as empty slates on which new knowledge should be "written." Creativity was not a requirement but rather some quirk that had to be educated out of learners.

Since then education failed to keep up with the changing social and work environment. In a world where computing power doubles every 18 months and new knowledge follows in its slipstream, everything that we know today will represent only 1% of the world's body of knowledge before the end of the next decade. At the same time the nature of work is changing as the economic emphasis shifts toward a knowledge-based industry. Knowledge workers are the new elite and already in such short supply that people with specialized knowledge can virtually travel the global village without visas. They are prized for their constant stream of new ideas and their ability to work, either on their own without supervision, or interdependently as members of specialized ad hoc teams consisting of people from diverse cultures.

Even the nature of knowledge is changing: where former generations considered knowledge as eternal verities that, once acquired, would never lose their value, knowledge in the "new economy" simply means information packaged as marketable commodities. Yesterday's cutting-edge knowledge could therefore become tomorrow's stupidity.

This reality necessitates a serious rethinking of what schools should teach and how it should be done. The information era—in which the world now finds itself—requires people to be self-driven, to create their own jobs, and to solve problems creatively. In a rapidly changing world, workers will be compelled to change *careers* between three to seven times in a lifetime, and today's job seekers will probably retire in a career that does not even exist. Permanent jobs will become scarce worldwide. Contract work will be the rule and tenured careers the exception. In the next twenty years factories will most likely require only 15% of their present labor force. As a result everybody will be responsible for his or her own job opportunities and doing his or her own marketing.

We will all need to become self-reliant, critical thinkers endowed with the necessary skills to solve problems creatively in order to survive. As the author of this book puts it:

> A partial list of these quality-thinking processes could include transformational thinking, global awareness, systemic thinking, recognizing relationships, visionary futuristic thinking, intuitive and paradoxical thought, and critical thinking as defined in recent studies. The complex, dynamic nature of the times demands new kinds of thinking and problem-solving everywhere . . .

Bee Bleedorn has spent a lifetime experimenting, lobbying, and thinking of ways in which the education system could be improved. That brought her to the following conclusion:

> All humans have an inherent urge to learn and to grow, to enhance themselves, and to be recognized as significant in some way. The process of delivering learning is complicated by the fact that humans differ in their basic learning and thinking styles. Assessing achievement only on the basis of standardized tests is a serious limitation to the evaluation of student learning. Unless creativity, empathy, flexibility, vision, global awareness, tolerance for ambiguity, and ethical standards are taught and modeled by teachers, standardized test scores may be high but application of skills and knowledge may fail application for positive human future development, both individually and collectively.

Intellectual arrogance, one could almost call it fundamentalism, has already brought the world to the verge of eco-collapse. According to Robert B. Shapiro of Monsanto, it is no longer possible to throw more "stuff" at the environment. Whatever problems we have, like food shortages and environmental imbalances, will have to be solved by knowledge and creative thinking. "A closed system, such as the earth's eco-system will not be able to withstand a systematic onslaught of an increase of material things, but it could even support an exponential increase in information and knowledge."

Whereas the educational system emanating from the Industrial Revolution was a great equalizer of people, the new system needs to accept that, just as we need bio-diversity in order to survive as a global eco-system, we need diversity of thinking talents and thinking styles to survive as a human race. As Dr. Bleedorn puts it:

> The natural resources of the world . . . may be finite; the human mind is the one resource that has unlimited possibility for development and contribution to a better world for more of its people. It is incumbent on education to design the twelve years spent in school for maximum growth and development of the potential of every student.

For Bee Bleedorn the key to a better future is to grow people: self-reliant, creative people with "heart":

> I have watched countless students at all levels of education change their attitude from apathetic to involved when they learn to trust the teacher's invitation for an expression of their creative ideas and when a classroom climate guarantees respect for diversity from their peers. The relationship between self-concept, antisocial behavior, and criminality has been the subject of study and speculation for a long time. It is not difficult to believe that if a person is denied the privilege of expression, he can be expected to express himself in a drive for power and identity, often of a negative kind.

The positive contribution of every citizen according to his ability is what makes democracy work.

In this she agrees with the great Venezuelan pioneer, Dr. Luis Alvaro Machado, who believes that intelligent and creative people are a prerequisite for stable democracy:

> Everybody has, simply by existing, a right to be intelligent. And to be provided with a way to become consistently more intelligent. This is a right that must be recognized and held sacred. Above all, the necessary conditions for the exercise of this right must be available; this is society's mission and the primary obligation of its leaders, all of them. (Machado, *The Right to Be Intelligent*)

Dr. Bleedorn's book is not simply "another book" on education, but rather a book that is in many ways definitive about the role of creativity and thinking skills in education. This book is not only meant for educators, but deserves a broad audience and should, moreover, be compulsory reading for all policy makers.

— Dr. Piet Muller, M.A., Ph.D.
Founder and Chairman, sDr. P. J. Muller and Associates
Pretoria, South Africa

Acknowledgments

THE IDEA OF promoting the deliberate and specific teaching of creative and other quality thinking processes throughout the formal educational experience has become a personal preoccupation. The many years of independent leadership in the exploration and teaching of creative thinking began gradually to point to a broader mission when it became clear that radical changes in the world and its human affairs began to demand a new kind of thinking. Acquaintance with the academic world from many perspectives resulted in an awareness of the need for a more integrative, holistic system for serving the educational needs of a diverse student population in the process of learning and preparation for life and service in a democracy. A shift from the industrial age to the information age, new global realities, and concerns for environmental sustainability were additional factors in the formula for educational change. The idea became a professional journey.

Many individuals contributed to the years of independent study, reflection, and hard work that culminated in the message in this book. Many of those contributors provided a supportive presence in my life and work. Many others, through their vision and inspired writing, became unwitting contributors. I could never remember them all, but I will try.

Dr. E. Paul Torrance, who started me on the creativity track at the University of Minnesota and remained a cherished friend and mentor through all the years.

J. P. Guilford, who provided the theoretical structure of intellect, which led me to recognize the order of complexity in products of thought and gave me the argument for adding other quality thinking to the current efforts for academic attention to creative thinking.

Harlan Cleveland, who opened my "doors of perception" to include the global dimensions and establish confidence in the possibilities of new kinds of leadership in the world's future.

Piet Muller, creative professional leader and philosopher of South Africa, who, in spite of his demanding schedule took the time to review the text for this book and to give it a foreword. I am so grateful for his friendship and wisdom.

Frank Maraviglia, State University of New York Syracuse, whose conversations and professional collaborations were a source of energetic ideas and encouragement.

Josef Mestenhauser, whose authenticity and scholarship are leading the way to global education and the reforming of the higher education curriculum, and whose encouragement provided valuable motivation.

Patience Dirkx, for her wisdom and counsel along with her comprehensive and always available help with the mysteries and vagaries of the computer.

Gary Jedynak, who with an uncommon scope of understanding and experience generously provided his constant support and service from the very beginning.

Efiong Etuk, a valued colleague, whose "Insights on Human Creativity" proved inspiring and profoundly encouraging to my way of thinking.

Lynne Krause, executive director of the American Creativity Association, whose enthusiastic response to my first book of readings encouraged the creation of this second book.

Earl Belide, University of St. Thomas, St. Paul, Minnesota, reference library specialist, whose library skills and good will were always available.

The lieutenant governor of Minnesota, Mae Schunk, whose recognition of my commitment to education afforded me an opportunity to share ideas as a member of her education advisory committee.

Garnet Millar, Torrance biographer and collaborator, whose scholarship and friendship keep me in touch with developments in the work of E. Paul Torrance and the Center for Creativity at the University of Georgia.

Marie Manthey, founder and president emeritus of the corporation Creative Health Care Management, who has been an encouragement by honoring my work in her promotion of my first book of readings throughout her corporation.

United Nations Association of Minnesota board of directors and chairman Arlen Erdahl, where the meetings constantly reinforce my vision of global realities and education.

A collection of creative thinkers from diverse perspectives who gather regularly at "a meeting of minds" for the pleasure of thinking across labels and boundaries, and who listen with interest to my updates on developments in the discipline of creativity.

An unlimited assortment of friends and colleagues who have been on hand with their support and encouragement for any number of initiatives on creativity. The list includes Steve Dahlberg, Robin Eggum, Tracy Leverentz, Bob Clyde, John Neville, Barbara Schroedl, Shirley Graczyk, Fins Peterson, Mary Patterson, Marie Thielen, Margaret Petersen, and many more.

Finally, my daughters, Joan Barnes and Bonnie Sample, turned their considerable computer skills and abundant human spirit toward the final formatting and organizing of the manuscript. Despite their own busy schedules, they worked together in a grand display of teamwork to meet the submission date.

Also, I am profoundly grateful for all the public officials and political leaders who distinguish themselves by the complex quality of their thinking, their inspired words, and their courageous leadership.

For all of these and many more I offer most sincere and everlasting gratitude.

Introduction

⑥
A Personal Reflection

SOME SERIOUS THINKING persuaded me that the best introduction to this collection of articles would be a reflective statement of my personal journey of academic exploration and discovery. It is a record that accounts for the scope and intensity of my belief system regarding creative education.

My earliest teaching experience in a Minnesota rural school to a doctorate and university professorship (with a brief detour as consultant with the Minnesota Department of Education) centered on the dynamics of student learning and thinking. Studies in educational psychology with Dr. E. Paul Torrance at the University of Minnesota in the mid-sixties introduced me to the discipline of creativity and provided the theoretical base for the intuitive perceptions and practices of creative education that had marked my student-oriented teaching style from the beginning. I fall into the category of educators described by Harlan Cleveland as "a reflective practitioner and a practical academic" (Cleveland, 1998).

Years of association with creativity programs and institutes, a penchant for independent study, and a sense of mission to provide academic leadership in establishing attention and legitimacy to creative studies all contributed to a 35-five year history of teaching, lecturing, writing, and educational entrepreneurship in the field of creativity.

Three major authorities in the understanding of human thought and behavior significantly influenced the ideas presented here. Dr. E. Paul Torrance became my mentor during my studies at the Department of Educational Psychology at the University of Minnesota. The intensity of his educational commitment, his pioneering spirit, and his profound respect and encouragement for students set guidelines that I used all of my professional life. A recent biography testifies to the extent and influence of his leadership (Millar, 1995). Another constant guide for the understanding of human differences and possibilities was an early acquaintance with J. P. Guilford and his model of the Structure of Intellect. His presentation to the American Psychological Association in 1959 opened the doors to the understanding and development of the creativity discipline and formed the basis for subsequent work on multi-intelligences by authorities such as Howard Gardner and Arnold Skromme. A third major influence on the nature of the articles is the seminal work on leadership by James MacGregor Burns whose ideas I encountered in studying leadership and human behavior at U.S. International University in San Diego in 1985. The factor of global dimensionality is drawn from an acquaintance with and admiration for the thinking of Harlan Cleveland, founder and first director of the Humphrey Institute of Public Affairs at the University of Minnesota.

Because the creative thinking process applies across all disciplines, I became an early advocate for interdisciplinary studies and integrative education. As an older student and later as a member of university faculties I found other reasons to look for changes in higher education programs and practices. Traditional academic emphasis on the behavioristic, quantitative research orientation of the behavioral sciences and years of delay in the official validation of humanistic, qualitative research by behavioral sciences added necessity to a natural curiosity and inclination for independent learning.

Years of exploring the serious literature on creativity and related philosophies, along with active involvement in conferences with relevance to creativity provided valuable resources for participating in the evolution of the discipline of creative education, defined recently in its broadest sense as:

> an approach to learning and human development that is primarily concerned with helping each learner recognize his unique talents and, then, providing him with

relevant experiences, facilities, and resources (including academic skills) to strengthen and, eventually, engage his natural abilities in things that he perceives as important and beneficial to himself, his employer, and his society. (Etuk, 2002)

A natural extension of that discipline leads to the promotion of the deliberate teaching of other quality thinking processes. Science and technology provide the means for the immediate acquisition of unlimited quantities of information. Now, however, we also recognize the need for development and practice of higher quality processes of thinking in tune with the global dimensions of a dynamic, complex world and its preservation.

A dramatic increase in the amount of literature and research relating to creativity connects it with a variety of issues of human potential and behavior, including self-concept, higher consciousness, humor, learning styles, prison populations, brain hemispheric dominance, spirituality, and leadership. Ervin Laszlo, writing in the *Noetic Sciences Review*, reminded readers that, "a new consciousness is already surfacing at the creative edge of our society. A quiet but significant groundswell is building today, made up of people who are changing their preferences, priorities, values, and beliefs" (Laszlo, 2002).

My doctoral dissertation, published in 1988 by Peter Lang Inc., was titled, "Creative Leadership for a Global Future: Studies and Speculations." The research showed that of the talents perceived by educators, business leaders, and college students to be of primary importance for global, futuristic leadership, a majority were not perceived to be adequately addressed in current American educational practices (Bleedorn, 1988).

⑥

Connections

Studies at an international university and constant contacts with students from all over the world opened my perception of global and futuristic trends. Connections to an already established focus on creative studies are continuing to emerge. The fact is becoming increasingly obvious that, despite the diversity of humans, human affairs in the global village are irrevocably interdependent. This interconnection and the dynamics of a radically changing planetary family demand a new level of systemic, visionary thinking on the part of both leaders and followers.

As a teacher of creative studies and futures studies in both graduate education and business/entrepreneurship departments, and later as lecturer/trainer in creative studies for the business community, I became aware of the need for stronger relationships and connections between the institution of education and the "real world" of business. The case for their mutual interest in the "creative force" is laid out in my 1998 publication, *The Creativity Force in Education, Business, and Beyond: An Urgent Message* (Bleedorn, 1998). A recent article in *The Washington Monthly* (Florida, 2002) testifies to the trend in business that depends on "the creative class" to contribute to economic development.

Schools always took on the responsibility of preparing citizens in a democracy to participate and contribute to the common good as well as to their own personal growth and development. Recognizing and cultivating creative thinking and problem-solving talents, along with other higher quality thinking processes should be an essential part of the current public and political attention to educational reform.

Institutions and organizations are all best served with habits of thought connected to the creative process as it relates to high-capability thinking, including systemic thought, integrative thought, vision, the unity of diversities, and paradoxical thought and transformation. These organizations, such as The World Future Society, Global Education Associates, United Nations Chapter, Creative Education Foundation, World Peace Movement, American Creativity Association, environmental organizations, all strive to remind members of their relationship to processes of quality thinking.

The ideals of peace and justice in the world, the quality of life, and maybe even the survival of our planetary home depend upon the evolution of the mind to higher, more complex levels. Schools everywhere have an obligation to direct specific attention to quality thinking in official curricula at all levels.

❧

A Collection

The articles collected here represent a variety of perspectives, most of which argue for a more serious academic attention on the part of educators everywhere to the discipline of creativity and the teaching of creativity and other quality thinking processes up, down, and sideways in school programs. The scope of my interests in the application of creativity concepts has been broad. The articles in the collection reflect that scope. No special effort was made to follow a standard pattern in the nature and focus of the individual articles. Rather, they represent a somewhat random reminder of the broad diversity of human experience that depends upon the thinking and the collective wisdom of everyone involved.

The time frame of the articles lacks a certain consistency. In some cases clear evidence shows that arguments and efforts for educational change made earlier have had a limited measure of attention in official academe. The facts continue to apply. Application of theories and practices advanced by early authorities like Torrance, Guilford, Burns, and Cleveland are more likely to depend upon dedicated scholars and advocates than on the established hierarchical system of traditional leadership. Changes in education are happening in private schools, in experimental and charter schools, and in regular classrooms where entrepreneurial teachers find ways to exercise the freedom to teach, but the pattern of official educational establishment awaits sincere commitment from the top down to new ways of thinking about learning and its administration.

❧

Purpose and Audience

Conversations with serious educators at all levels, as well as with serious thinkers throughout society find ready agreement with the idea that everyone has individual learning needs, a natural urge to learn, to grow, to enhance oneself, and a hope to be recognized for some special talent. Large, inflexible, tightly organized and categorized systems of management fail to sufficiently allow for student diversities and freedom of thought. The basic purpose of this collection of readings is threefold.

1. To argue that if educators are serious about reform related to the changing times, they will teach in ways that recognize and cultivate the highest thinking capability of all students, both in the student's own personal behalf and as an intellectual resource critical for human capacities to meet the challenges of social change and the preservation of our planetary home.

2. To rally the educational and social forces to give to every learner the right to understand instead of simply to learn; to be perceived as an individual with distinct learning and thinking styles within the context of developmental stage theory as advanced early on by Gowan (1972) and Piaget (1950); and especially the right and freedom to think independently, and to express those ideas and have them respected. A just society requires that this right be protected.

3. To remind the reader that the deliberate teaching of thinking processes does not preclude the traditional teaching of content and basic skills. In fact the art of creative and related thinking processes enhances the internalization and motivation for all learning. The integration can be described as "learning to think; thinking to learn."

The hope for this collection is that the diversity and interrelatedness of ideas in the articles will find a readership, both public and academic, that responds to the message. Harlan Cleveland, former founder and director of the Humphrey Institute for Reflective Leadership at the University of Minnesota often suggested that change generally comes not so much from top, official places, but "bubbles up" from the bottom. Growing evidence indicates that those concerned with the education of children and youth and with effective leadership for a new and challenging kind of interrelated world—educators, parents, public officials, and world leaders—all are ready for new ways of thinking about what we teach and how we teach it.

◎

Summary

The human family is on the brink of major shifts. The new directions depend upon the attitudes, values, and combined thinking of both designated and undesignated leaders. The first step in change is awareness. These essays are designed to articulate the following conclusions:

1. The creative force is present in all humans to some degree. Pressures to conform within education and society often silence creative expression for many students and citizens. The potential for its development remains, however.

2. The human brain/mind, with its unlimited growth and possibilities, is the most powerful resource available for managing a society in transition. Thinking processes need to be better recognized, understood, and developed in institutionalized learning.

3. The academic discipline of creative studies teaches the understanding of creative persons, the creative process, the creative product, and creative press (environment for the encouragement of creative expression).

4. Studies of creativity lead naturally to the teaching of other quality thinking processes (critical thinking, problem solving, recognizing relationships, awareness of systems and one's place within the "big picture," integrative thinking, a capacity for vision and having some time reality in the future, the art of paradoxical thinking, and more).

5. Students, citizens, and their institutions are all in need of new patterns of thinking for meeting the challenges of change. Education at all levels, including higher education, and especially teacher education departments would do well to start at the top of the established learning ladder and shift its paradigm by adding the teaching of quality thinking processes to the traditional diet of learning, remembering, and finding the "right answer," which may

no longer be the best answer for an integrated planetary family in transition.

It is time to acknowledge the educational experience as a process that results in more than certification for a better job and greater income and status. It is time for all of society to perceive the years of institutionalized learning as a preparation for individuals to develop their natural intellectual talents, which would provide a base for lifetime learning. It is a time for the cultivation of high capability, quality, complex thinking as a contributing member of the human family. A long time ago Oliver Wendell Holmes made the following observations.

> There are one-story intellects, two-story intellects, and three-story intellects with skylights. All fact-collectors who have no aim beyond their facts are one-story men. Two-story men compare, reason, generalize, using the labor of the fact-collectors as their own. Three-story men idealize, imagine, predict—their best illumination comes from above through the skylight.

CHAPTER 1

Education for a Just Society: Freedom to Think

In the rapid transformation produced by globalization and informitization, the role of the individual is crucial. Individual creativity must unfold to its fullest extent, and it can unfold only if the individual has the optimum—which is never the maximum—freedom of thought, expression and action . . . encouraging the creativity of individuals and enabling the fruits of such creativity to penetrate to the full social organism. For this reason freedom in thinking, in expression, and in action is a paradigmatic requirement of transition to a just global society.

— *Laszlo, 1992*

AT THE FIRST International Dialogue on Transition to a Global Society in 1990, the influence of education on the world problematique was a recurring theme. Frederico Mayor (1990) called for a global approach to "engender the necessary change in thinking particularly within the educational system, as well as in social, political, scientific, and cultural affairs," and suggested that the time for action (worldwide "perestroika") had arrived. Ilya Prigogine spoke of "freeing ourselves" from old patterns of thinking and aiming instead at a "new utopia" (Prigogine, 1990).

Implicit in these remarks was the genuine issue of human potential and the evolution of human intellect in educational planning everywhere in the emerging world order. The ideals of liberty, equality, and fraternity apply to all persons or they apply to none in the global schema. This discussion focuses not on acknowledged differences, but on the common human potential for what William Blake speaks of as "opening the doors of perception" to new, more visionary, creative

1

habits of mind. Educational purposes and possibilities will need major rethinking if learners are to prepare for participation and leadership in the paradigm shift to greater democratization in the world.

Although the concept of changing patterns of thinking does, admittedly, present a universal educational challenge, the practices and possibilities of such a change are gaining momentum. Strategies for the deliberate teaching of creative and critical thinking, of problem solving, of paradoxical and systemic futuristic thinking are all becoming part of educational reform. But not fast enough.

This discussion is intended (1) to argue for the importance of understanding, teaching, and practicing the full range of human thinking potential as a fundamental force for the transition to a just society and (2) to report examples of developments in the "politics of ideas" and actions that are providing leadership in education and business, especially in the growing attention to the teaching of creative thinking.

⑥

Thinking Process for a Just Society

Some time ago I attended a showing of two documentary films that related quite directly to the issue of justice. One film reported the trial and sentencing of a Native American accused of shooting a U.S. officer on a reservation in South Dakota. The other reported a union/management dispute and strike at a meat packing plant in a small town in Minnesota. Viewing them was a powerful reminder of the human urge for justice and the value conflicts inherent in the process of transition to a just society. Tensions between a sense of justice and personal self-interest contribute to difficulties in perceptions and negotiations. Both of the films reinforce the impression that much of human behavior demonstrates an inability of the popular mind to think beyond absolutes and polarizations of opposites to a more empathic unity of differences. Decisions based on preconceived assumptions and prejudices fall short of the mark of justice whenever, wherever, and by whatever gender decisions are made or behavior is determined.

U Thant of Burma, Secretary General of the United Nations from 1961 to 1979, recognized the obligation of educational systems in the teaching of higher-level thinking processes. He argues especially for the development of the process of thinking at the level of paradox.

> I consider that the primary task of the educationist everywhere is to dispel certain age-old assumptions. It seems to be assumed, for example, that there are no more than two sides to a problem. As a matter of fact, almost every problem has more than two sides. It is also fallacious to paint human beliefs and human societies in terms of pure black and white. There are various shades in between; and there are human common-alities. Problems of racism and intolerance for differences could be reduced if attitudes and behavior had the benefit of a level of thinking that looks for those various shades in between. (U Thant, 1963)

As early as 1979, Botkin, Elmandjra, and Malitza, in a report to the International Club of Rome, called attention to the "dichotomy between a growing complexity of our own making and a lagging development of our own capacities" (Botkin et al., 1979). The Club of Rome is an international group of scientists, educators, and government leaders concerned with the enormous problems of energy, food, and population. The demands of future leadership and responsible participation in a pluralistic global society require new understandings, new perceptions, new skills, new behaviors, and critical to all the rest, new ways of thinking together. The Earth Summit meeting in Rio de Janeiro in June 1992 brought into focus the thought of our common humanity and the universally shared hope for a just and peaceful world.

Common, also, to most cultures and religions is a maxim admonishing the people to behave toward others in ways that they would like others to behave toward them. Such common spiritual guidelines take on cosmic dimensions in a Native American definition quoted by

Charlotte Black Elk at a national Nobel Peace Conference at Gustavus Adolphus College in St. Peter, Minnesota: "God is a sphere, the center of which is anywhere and the circumference of which is everywhere." Albert Einstein, the scientist, said it this way:

> The more knowledge we acquire, the more mystery we find. A human being is part of the whole, called by us the Universe, a part limited in time and space. He experiences himself, his thoughts and feelings as something separate from the rest, a kind of optical illusion of his consciousness. This delusion is a kind of prison for us, restricting us to our personal desires and to affection for a few persons nearest us. Our task must be to free ourselves from this prison by widening our circle of compassion to embrace all living creatures and the whole of nature in its beauty. (Einstein, in McGaa, 1990)

The relevant role of education in society's transition is readily acknowledged. Designing education that deliberately creates thinking patterns supportive of a new, interrelated, fair, human, just global society is a staggering task. Beginning steps for such a "ministry of liberation" are already in place.

◈

Education and the Teaching of Thinking Processes

The deliberate teaching of creative and critical thinking processes as a crucial additive to the traditional teaching of content, skills, and "right answers" has increased in momentum during the 50 years since the establishment of the Creative Education Foundation at the University of New York in Buffalo. The Foundation has been the gathering place for leading authorities in the field of educational psychology, such as Dr. E. Paul Torrance, who has provided research and resources for identification, activation, and cultivation of the creative potential of students at all levels of education and throughout the adult community. The relationship between habits of mind and the need for a paradigm shift to more creative ways of thinking for the increasingly complex nature of human society is underscored in this statement:

> The genius of the future will be the creative mind adapting itself to the shape of things to come. This will require "Satori" bursts of new insights. The skills of creative thinking must be recognized as mankind's most important adaptability skills. Such skills must become basic to the curriculum of schools, homes, business, and other agencies. (Torrance, 1979)

Although critical thinking may seem to be the opposite side of the coin from creative thinking, the two processes are interrelated. Critical thinking has often been perceived in a negative sense, that is, the obligation to point out only the faults and weaknesses of new ideas, products, or procedures. In a more current and enlightened interpretation, a distinction is made between weak, narrow-minded critical thinking based on selfish and biased motivations, and strong, fair-minded critical thinking with an understanding of the total system and organizational goals. Strong, fair-minded critical thinking can be defined as the process of thinking clearly and accurately with a view to judging fairly. Higher levels of thinking that go beyond the immediate personal focus to a perception of the system and implications for the future can be creatively critical and critically creative. At that level, relationships operate on a mutualistic level and ethical thinking and decision making become possible.

⑥

Nature of the Discipline of Creativity

An accumulation of research studies provides insights and understanding that form the basis for the teaching of creativity. Traditionally, these studies addressed the factors of creative person, process, and product. Subsequently, the additional factor of "press" or the environment for creative, productive thinking and behaving became a critical consideration in creative teaching.

A major contribution to the understanding and development of the creative thinking process is the Torrance Tests of Creative Thinking, published by Scholastic Testing Service in Bensenville, Illinois. The tests, translated into more than 40 different languages and used in more than 2,000 research studies, measure four cognitive factors of creative thinking: fluency, flexibility, originality, and elaboration.

The discovery and practice of the creative talents for flexible thinking are particularly relevant for a diverse, pluralistic global society that is searching for *unity* in cultural and ideological differences. It has been said that "unity without diversity is uniformity; diversity without unity is chaos; justice is served when unity and diversity exist together in creative tension." Ervin Laszlo (1992) reminds us that the creative interplay of diversity and integration is a feature of the contemporary world with unparalleled relevance to the future of humanity. Without diversity, the parts could not form an entity capable of growth, development, and change. Without integration, the diverse elements could not become a dynamic, unitary structure.

Injustice and intolerance grow when human thinking processes are fixed on a single, preconditioned habit of mind based on superficial labels and prejudice. The recognition and practice of flexible thinking talents encourage the art of thinking at a level of paradox that, if readily available, would result in more understanding and less fighting. Love of homeland is not opposite, but is compatible with planetary citizenship. Genuine solidarity and respect for differences can coexist. It is time to acknowledge that concepts of war and injustice begin in the minds of men and women, and that the human family is overdue for a major mind change. Our common humanity can transcend the violence that comes from differences if people can be educated to become better thinkers. Edward de Bono (1992), international authority and teacher of creative thinking, believes that our methods of thinking are antiquated. Our style of argument was set up by the famous Greek gang of three—Socrates, Plato, and Aristotle. De Bono says that arriving at the truth by arguing and attacking each other's case is an extremely inefficient method of getting anywhere.

In addition to flexibility, the factor of originality in thinking processes is recognized and encouraged in the teaching of creativity at all levels of learning. Strategies for overcoming blocks to creative thinking imposed by conforming, standardized educational practices, cultures, emotions, and hostile environments stimulate the production of new ideas for solving problems and meeting challenges of change. The creative problem-solving process (Parnes, 1981) teaches the fundamental concept of deferred judgment throughout its five-step process. A mindset for allowing new ideas and alternative ways of being to be carefully considered before making critical judgments is a mindset for greater fairness in relationships and less prejudged polarization of opposites.

New problems and challenges call for new and original solutions. Society's escalating information base demands greater balance and equality with a thinking base that crosses the entire spectrum of human intellectual potential. The Guilford Model of the Structure of Intellect (Guilford, 1968), which gave momentum to the study of creative, divergent thinking, lists the products of thinking in ascending order of complexity: from units up through classes, relationships, systems, transformations, and finally, implications of the art of visionary thought.

Creative educational practices based on creative and critical thinking processes are turning more toward the metacognitive understanding of the variant powers of the mind, the limited use to which they have been put (15% by estimate), and the critical need for their greater activation. Fritjov Capra suggests that the most critical issues of our time have been

> excluded from the political dialogue because they cannot be adequately addressed within the current mode of thinking. Our present worldview is based on a perception of reality that has dominated our society for the past three hundred years and that has become institutionalized and vested with power, but that is now

incapable of conceiving new solutions. Ultimately, all
these problems are facets of one single crisis, which is
essentially a crisis of perception. (Capra, 1990)

Higher levels of perceiving and thinking about systems, transformations, and implications as presented by Guilford's Model are
teachable. The teaching of futures studies as advocated by the World
Future Society engages the highest level of thinking in terms of implications. Such a use of the mind makes possible the perception of things
to come based on recognizable present realities. Strategies for avoiding
perceived negative futures can help problem solving become proactive
rather than reactive.

In addition to the measurable factors in the cognitive domain of
creativity, the affective domain of the creative person relates to survival
and to making a contribution to a changing, complex world. Creative
qualities of independence of thought, risk taking, tolerance
for ambiguity, curiosity, and sensitivity mark the creative individuals
who might be described as "the conscience of the crowd." The
thoughtful minority voice with the standards of a mature conscience is
more often recognized as ethical, thoughtful, flexible, and fair in
judgment when strong differences and disruptions arise. Recognizing
and rewarding such qualities of mind where they already exist and
teaching paradoxical, systemic, visionary, and transformative thinking
processes to learners at all levels and in all educational programs
support the natural time-consuming evolutionary growth of human
intellect.

In fact, in discussing the psychology of man's possible evolution, the
philosopher P. D. Ouspensky wrote:

One fundamental idea shall be that man as we know
him is not a completed being; that nature develops him
only up to a certain point and then leaves him to
develop further by his own efforts and devices, or to live
and die such as he was born or to degenerate and lose
the capacity for development. Evolution of man [and

woman] in this case will mean the development of certain inner qualities and features that usually remain undeveloped and cannot develop by themselves. (Ouspensky, 1973)

⑥

Creative Trends in Universal Education

More than 20 years ago a report to the Club of Rome called attention to the "dichotomy between a growing complexity of our own making and a lagging development of our own capacities" (Botkin et al., 1979). Growing evidence indicates that the capacity to think creatively and at higher levels is beginning to be specifically addressed in learning opportunities at all levels and across the spectrum of education, business, and society in general. At the Creative Problem Solving Institute in Buffalo, New York, hundreds of participants from all over the world engage in the study and practices of creative and critical thinking from basic applications to extensions into general systems and transformation theories. Participants from Spain, South Africa, Norway, United Kingdom, Mexico, Brazil, Canada, Netherlands, China, Singapore, Chile, Italy, Middle East, and many other places engage in leadership of creative studies.

European conferences on creativity and innovation like the one in Nordwijk aan Zee in the Netherlands in 1991 attract participants from business, education, and general public. An International Creativity and Innovation Networking Conference is regularly held at the Center for Creative Leadership in Greensboro, North Carolina. National and international efforts promote the availability of resources for teaching creative thinking and problem solving in order to stimulate higher-level thinking in populations of gifted and talented students. Independent consultants worldwide provide training and development in the discipline of creativity for education, business, and general public.

In 2001 Winslow Press published the first "Creativity's Global Correspondents—2001," edited by Dr. Morris Stein. The collection of articles included works by authors from Germany, Hong Kong, Israel,

Poland, Portugal, Romania, Russia, Singapore, South Africa, Spain, Tanzania, Vietnam, United Kingdom, and the United States. The discipline of creativity is becoming an integrative force in efforts toward mutuality and understanding among nations in the global transition to new ways of thinking.

⑥

Educational Leadership for Creating Change

Arieti (1976) suggested that "whether it is considered from the viewpoint of its effects on society, or an expression of the human spirit, creativity stands out as an activity to be studied, cherished and cultivated." A great deal of talent important in the transition to a just, global society is lost when creative expression and potential of any person is discouraged or ignored. Characteristics of the creative individual identified in a study by MacKinnon (1978) include a high level of effective intelligence, an openness to experience, a freedom from crippling restraints and impoverishing inhibitions, an esthetic sensitivity, a cognitive flexibility, an independence in thought, unquestioning commitment to creative endeavor, and an unceasing striving for solutions to difficult problems. The demands of human participation in the advancing order of global complexity require new understandings, new perceptions, new skills, new behaviors, and critical to all the rest, new ways of thinking.

As is often the case, the role of education in the task of the transition to a just, global society is "long on diagnosis and short on prescription." The role of the educational entrepreneur, working to bring the teaching of creative, critical, and other higher orders of thinking into a valued place in academic programming, requires patience and persistence. It also requires courage, risk taking, and initiative. Colleges and universities organized around the structure of departmentalized, special fields based on content and skills find difficulty in integrating into the official curriculum the interdisciplinary nature of the teaching of thinking processes. The role of the change agent, especially in the structured, bureaucratic environment of many institutions of learning, relates well to Harlan Cleveland's analogy of the leader as the "first bird off the telephone wire" (Cleveland, 1984).

> Anyone who has seen the martins and swallows in September, assembling on the telephone wires, twittering, making short flights singly and in groups over the open, stubbly fields, returning to form long and even longer lines above the yellowing verges of the lanes—the hundreds of individual birds merging and blending, in a mounting excitement, into swarms, and these swarms coming loosely and untidily together to create a great, unorganized flock, thick at the center and ragged at the edges, which breaks and re-forms continually like clouds of waves—until that moment when the greater part (but not all) of them know that the time has come; they are off, and have begun once more that great southward flight which many will not survive; a kind of telepathic feeling has to flow through them and ripen to the point when they all know that they are ready to begin.

Because society's capacity for change depends upon the thinking capacity of individuals who make it up, enlightened universal education will have to foster learning that will produce planetary leadership talents, while at the same time protect the national and cultural diversities of the men and women in the global family. Although some of the planet's resources are finite, the reason for "unwarranted optimism" is that the human mind is unlimited in its capacity to think, to grow, to plan ahead, and to act in terms of the common good. The role of education is critical to this challenge. Could it be that education is getting ready to gather its forces for its leadership role in the creation of a more thoughtful and just society?

CHAPTER 2

What Shall We Teach and How Shall We Teach It?

*The principal goal of education is to create men and women
who are capable of doing new things, not simply of repeating
what other generations have done . . . men and women who
are creative, inventive discoverers. The second goal of education is to form minds which can be critical, can verify and
not accept everything they are offered.*

— *Jean Piaget*

THE ARGUMENT TO improve education by paying teachers more money
and cutting back class size may be the start of a new educational direction, but it's not the bottom-line direction. After salaries for teachers
are raised and class size lowered, the basic question remains for all
levels of formal learning from preschool all the way to graduate education. How shall we design institutionalized learning in ways that will
prepare citizens for a new kind of interrelated, interactive, complex
global society while at the same time preserve their cultural identity
and sense of place in the system? What shall we teach? How shall we
teach it? Who shall do the teaching?

As an educator with a lifetime of service all the way from rural school
teaching to an appointment in the Minnesota State Department of Education, I followed the crosshatch of trends and arguments for educational reform for many years. Based on that experience, I feel that some
critical issues should have a more public and prominent place in any
proposed plan for change.

What shall we teach? The basic skills as a starter and as tools for accomplishing the greater learning. Teaching the art of thinking with the
full range and potential of the brain/mind is a proper addition to the
list of basic skills. Creative and critical thinking, problem solving and

conflict resolution, global and futuristic thinking, systemic and para-doxical thought patterns are all of inestimable value for citizens of a democracy. The right to think should not be denied to anyone. No student should be left behind, but no student should be deprived of the right to move ahead and to develop to the highest possible in-dividual level of intellectual capacity. We have known for years how to teach thinking processes, but it needs a more visible place in all curricula.

Add to the teaching of thinking processes a more serious academic attention to the teaching of environmental studies, global futures, the United Nations and peace studies, cultural diversity and human be-havior, and certainly foreign language. Actually, new ways of thinking can be taught within the context of any subject matter. Which leads to the second question: *How shall it be taught?*

The natural integration of learning and thinking has never been adequately addressed. The inclination to structure education based on labels, categories, specialized fields, and a strict hierarchical organi-zational pattern with little provision for recognizing and practicing the integration of the separate parts into a total system limits quality thinking. Adequate attention to interdisciplinary studies and inte-grative teaching in programs of higher education is overdue.

In addition to the teaching of big-picture thinking, the application of basic principles of effective learning needs updating. A prime example is the strategy of connecting learning to a direct, purposeful experience. Especially for students whose learning style is concrete and random in nature, the tactile, hands-on experience engages the mind and facil-itates learning. The "Incubation Model of Teaching" originated by Dr. E. Paul Torrance, provides a guideline for teachers at any level.

Current excellent examples of school programs promote learning by taking a class into the real world of nature to make contact with its natural wonders. Based on their experiences, students can better practice a full range of basic skills and learning of content across the entire curriculum. Learning and growing is meant to be an exciting, stimulating activity. For many students experiential learning can change attitudes from apathy and boredom to serious engagement.

Finally, *who shall teach in our schools?* Those men and women who themselves show an appetite and aptitude for learning, who are well prepared in their understanding and application of what we know about individual differences and developmental levels, who are prepared to work hard, to make use of their creative talents in the classroom, and who can depend upon the respect, gratitude, and rewards of service are essential to the profession of education.

◊

Observations on the Importance of Creative and Critical Thinking Processes and Strategies as a Foundation for Effective Learning

These ideas are offered with the hope that readers will add their own observations to the list.

1. We have changed almost everything in the world except the way we think. Educating students to new ways of thinking in a complex, interrelated world is a basic challenge now and for the future.

2. Higher levels of thinking, according to the Guilford Model of the Structure of Intellect, include thinking in systems, in relationships, in transformations, and in implications beyond the simple learned, memorized, right answer response.

3. The discipline of creative studies is an accumulation of more than 40 years of study, research, and practice related to the discipline of educational psychology and the full use of the human capacity to think and to solve problems.

4. Creative and critical thinking processes can be formally and specifically taught and integrated into the teaching of any subject matter. Methods and materials are constantly being developed. Students respond enthusiastically to a climate of organized freedom for the development and expression of their own advanced levels of thought and speculation.

5. Schools have a responsibility to develop more effective ways of teaching thinking skills to more students if this country is to compete in the world of new ideas and products.

6. New thinking begins with a critique of old thinking. An article by Sheila Tobias in *Change* suggests that some 300 reports on the problem of American science and mathematics education have been issued since 1983 (May/June 1992). Yet it is "hard to show that these reports have had much impact." Real change requires a paradigm shift to new ways of thinking and learning.

7. Conventionally conditioned teachers show a reluctance to give up the familiar teaching that maintains their position of authority and control in favor of more open-ended inquiry and discovery methods that stimulate independent creative and critical thinking and excite the minds of learners.

8. Real learning, especially for certain learning styles, is best internalized when based on direct, purposeful experiences that can lead students to understandings of abstract concepts, patterns systems, and new connections.

9. When official change in educational programming occurs, it usually originates in local commitment where money finds its way directly into instruction.Traditional-based teachers can be helped to incorporate creative and critical thinking experiences into more effective and rewarding teaching.

10. The critical nature of threats to our global environment and the shared responsibility of citizen stewardship provide excellent motivation and opportunities for hands-on creative learning experiences in the real world and for teaching across the disciplines with attention to their integrative nature.

11. In the ideal learning environment that perceives the student as subject, new knowledge about individual learning and thinking styles underscores the need for a diversity of teaching methods. Students who, by their nature, are highly creative in thinking and behavior patterns are best served when learning is perceived as relevant and intellectually stimulating. Students who distinguish themselves academically and on standardized tests need experiences in the use of "whole brain" thinking that includes creative production of original ideas.

12. Growing attention to the seven intelligences identified by Howard Gardner of Harvard University is a reminder of the limitations of

IQ scores in identifying talents and strengths of individual students. Many of the brightest, most complex thinkers and imaginators are unrecognizable by traditional means, as well as often misunderstood and lost to the system and society. The new age needs their talents recognized and developed in whatever special way they excel.

13. The discipline of creative studies is attracting more and more sensitive, enlightened, and concerned educators. Balancing the teaching of thinking processes with the teaching of basic skills and content provides a formula that is long overdue. It is too important to be left to chance. Bold new initiatives and models for teaching a diversity of learners are high priority, and dedicated educators are positioned to provide leadership necessary for their accomplishment.

14. It has been said that many Americans grow up to be "science illiterates" who lack a working vocabulary of scientific terms and concepts, an understanding of how observations and experiments test our models of reality, and how important it is to understand the relationship between science and society.

15. It could be that a lack of scientific understanding renders voters and officials alike unable to make reasonable judgments on environmental issues. Creative teaching and learning provides thinking practices in forming and testing hypotheses, interpreting results, and drawing conclusions. A creative mind enjoys observing, speculating, and planning courses of action. Teaching creatively sets teachers free to design lessons and programs suitable for their particular group of students, based on current and meaningful content, integrative and collaborative.

16. Educational, business, and community programs nationally and internationally are incorporating leadership in the discipline of creativity. The Creative Education Foundation in Buffalo, New York, has provided international leadership for almost 50 years. Gradually, the myth that creativity resides exclusively in the arts is giving way to the reality that creativity is a natural and essential part of human identity and a benchmark of a responsible life experience.

17. Thinking patterns learned through the holistic system of the natural world in creatively effective science and mathematics classes transfer and integrate well with other areas of learning and living.
18. Resources and materials on creative teaching strategies from the work of authorities like E. Paul Torrance provide effective guidelines for classroom teachers in developing original and timely learning experiences.
19. A computer specialist with interest and insights into environmental studies as a real-world vehicle for teaching and learning could be an important resource in the preparation of programs and specific curricula for effective, reality-based learning.
20. Transition to a reasonable peaceful global society requires global citizens with a capacity for creative, critical, systemic thinking. It is happening, but not fast enough.

CHAPTER 3

The Environmental Brain:
System for Thinking and Learning

The mind can be permanently profaned by the habit of attending to trivial things, so that all our thought shall be tinged with triviality.

— *Henry David Thoreau*

SOONER OR LATER it will occur to serious thinkers (maybe it already has) that we are all a part of the natural world—interdependent and irrevocably interrelated. Not only is the natural world a living, changing evolving system, it is also an authentic model for the art of understanding the quality of thinking that focuses on the big picture rather than on its separate pieces. Lester Milbrath in his book on environmental thinking, admonishes us to think systemically, as opposed to systematically, if we would practice a mental process appropriate for the complexities of global realities.

> Systems thinkers focus on wholes rather than on parts. Within wholes they concern themselves with relationships more than objects, with process more than structures, with networks more than hierarchies. In a system, a given effect not only radiates through the system, it also feeds back and changes the factor that caused it. (Milbrath, 1996)

In the efforts of education to update the learning process to include the deliberate teaching of quality thinking, a powerful model could be found in the examples of interrelated parts of the organic scientific environment (Yau, 2002). It would be a natural step from observations and understandings of biological systems to the practice of systemic thinking in every other content of study.

A breakthrough concept in the understanding of the scope and diversity of human intellect (Guilford, 1977) provides the argument for the cultivation of systems thinking through environmental studies. The Guilford Model of the Structure of Intellect is presented in the form of a three-dimensional block. One dimension represents five possible contents of thought. Another dimension represents five alternative processes that act upon any of the contents. The third dimension is hierarchical in levels of complexity of six different possible products of thought. They are, in order of complexity from lowest to highest: Units, Classes, Relationships, Systems, Transformations, and Implications. (See figure 3.1.)

The following matrix provides the factors in the three dimensions of the model:

Content	Operations	Products
Figural	Memory	Units (least complex)
Auditory	Cognition	Classes
Semantic	Convergent thinking	Relationships
Symbolic	Divergent Thinking	Systems
Behavioral	Evaluative Thinking	Transformations
		Implications (most complex)

Any one of the content areas can be operated on by any one of the operations to arrive at any one of the products of thought. In this way the model identifies 150 different combinations or 150 ways of being smart. Although the content and operations dimensions are described as equal in levels of complexity, the products are arranged in a descending order of intellectual energy required. The concern here is with the position of systems represented as ranking higher than units, classes, and relationships.

Teaching that requires only perceptions of single units, classes, and relationships in any of the content and operations areas fails to challenge learners to think at a level of systems. It limits the potential

Figure 3.1 • 150 Ways to Use Your Brain

The Structure of Intellect

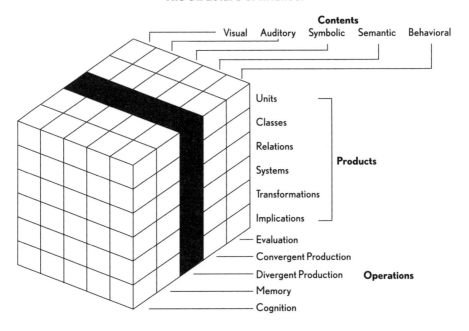

Products of Thought = A Hierarchy

LOW COMPLEXITY:	**Units**—Single Thing
	Classes—Label—Categorize
	Relations—Sameness—Differences—Cause and effect
	Systems—Holistic—Interactive realities (environment)
	Transformations—Creating and responding to Change
HIGH COMPLEXITY:	**Implications**—Some time reality in the future

Source: Guilford, J. P., *Way Beyond the I.Q.* (Buffalo, NY: Creative Education Foundation, Inc., 1977).

of the brain/mind to rise to the level of thought required of the inter-dependent global system. Speaking of "The Dangers of Education," Orr (1994) suggests that, "Many of the educational reforms now being proposed have little to do with the goals of personal wholeness, or the pursuit of truth and understanding, and even less to do with the great issues of how we might live within the limits of the earth. The reformers aim to produce people whose purposes and outlook are narrowly economic, not to educate citizens and certainly not citizens of the biotic community." Problems of the environment will get much worse if we don't change the way we think and act. A curriculum that fails to include deliberate attention to student involvement in systems thinking runs the risk of wasting mental talents needed for a satisfying, productive life and for leadership in the future of the earth and its people.

The intense efforts of environmentalists to preserve the finite resources of the world need to be matched with vigorous educational efforts to preserve and capitalize on the highest possible levels of human thought in its citizens. The good news is that there are no limits to learning (Botkin, 1979) and, we might add, to the satisfaction of getting smarter.

In his address at Chautauqua, New York, in 2001 on "Envisioning a Sustainable Environment," Lester Milbrath suggested that a love of nature was a reflection of a love of learning, and that humankind was going to have to learn its way to a new society. This argument might find a more powerful and profound expression in the maxim that we are going to have to *think* our way to a new world. Education does not have the luxury of ignoring its responsibility to lead the way in teaching and modeling holistic, futuristic thinking. The simple, mechanistic thinking of a traditional society is a denial of the laws of nature. According to Milbrath, ecological thinking relies on three basic guidelines for realistic, holistic, futuristic planning:

1. Waste matter and energy does not disappear. "Everything must go somewhere."
2. We can never do only one thing. (What else happened?)
3. Continue to ask, "And then what?"

A few provocative and relevant questions are posed by Orr.

> Could it be that the integrity, stability, and beauty of nature, however clever, is in fact a war against the source of mind? Could it be that the systematic homoge-

8

nization of nature inherent in contemporary technology and economics is undermining human intelligence? Can it be that we are in fact becoming both
more clever and less intelligent? If so, why is this?
(1994)

The search for understanding and solutions to questions of intelligence
and its importance, especially to democratic societies where citizens
have an obligation for informed voting, is ever present. Many years ago
William Blake gave us clues about opening the doors of perception. He
suggested that the first level of perception was sensory, and that suc-
ceeding levels of abstract, imaginative, and visionary thinking all de-
pended upon previous levels. His insight makes an argument for
teaching based upon organic, sensory encounters with the real world as
a base for the understanding of abstract, imaginative, and visionary perceptions or knowledge. In a much later discussion Fantini and Weinstein (1969) presented their model of a "Cone of Experience," suggesting that learning, especially for those with an inherent concrete
learning style, was better internalized when based upon a "direct, purposeful experience."

The teaching of environmental studies is uniquely designed for
direct, purposeful, sensory experiences in the world of nature. Concepts
of interrelationships, systems, interdependence, and human responsibility for future developments derive from observations and reflections
on environmental processes. The effective teaching of reading, writing,
math, science, and everything in-between through field trips puts
students in touch with the beauty and curiosities of their world,
followed by the stimulation and motivation for further study and
learning. For those so inclined, experiences in the presence of the
earth's wonders can lift thinking to a level of deeper awareness and
higher consciousness.

Former President Clinton in a talk at the University of California,
Berkeley, spoke of global interdependence.

Philosophers and theologians have long talked about
the interdependence of humanity. Politicians have

> talked about it quite seriously since the end of World War II, when the United Nations was established. But now ordinary people take it as a given because it pervades every aspect of our lives. We live in a world where we have torn down walls, collapsed distances and spread information. (Clinton, 2002)

A popular book recently appeared on the market, and attracted a great deal of attention: *The Cultural Creatives: How 50 Million People Are Changing the World* (Ray and Anderson, 2000). It is surprising to note that nowhere in the index is there a reference to *education*. Does its absence mean that changing the world is a project of the marketplace with no connection to the influence of education on the minds and attitudes of the population? At least it suggests that perceiving the interrelatedness of our social and political institutions has been outside of our level of awareness and that education has little or nothing to do with the total system of "changing the world."

The counterpart of studies of environmental systems can be found in concepts related to global education. The new realities of global communication, global commerce, global politics, and global environmental issues demand thinking of an order beyond the usual products of units, classes, and relationships. The demand is for expanded use of the brain's vast untapped potential and all the new ways to apply levels of systemic, visionary thinking appropriate to a complex society. Theories of right- and left-brain hemisphere dominance (Buzan, 1993) have associated systemic thinking with "right brain" as opposed to "left brain" sequential thinking. Communicating ideas systemically depends upon right-brain processes of mind mapping, a strategy highly effective for expressing interrelationships of the parts of a total system. Perceptions of environmental systems lend themselves well to mind mapping (Buzan, 1993). Establishing a habit of systemic thinking serves the complexities of a society in transition.

Institutions of higher education have good reason to reexamine their organizational structure to better serve systemic learning and thinking. Leadership with an integrative, environmental brain in a dynamically interconnected world becomes increasingly critical as global complexities grow. The separate nature of absolute academic disciplines and departments in university programs fails to develop interdisciplinary thinking across specializations. Habits of thought for which students are rewarded need to include evidence of the integration of special fields, which enriches the understanding of separate disciplines as well as of systems.

If schools were designed to produce scholars like Leonardo da Vinci, they would provide opportunity for the development of the Seven Da Vincian Principles (Gelb, 1998):

1. Curiosity and an insatiable quest for learning
2. A commitment to test knowledge through experience and risk-taking
3. Continual refinement of the senses
4. Willingness to embrace ambiguity, paradox, and uncertainty
5. Development of balance between science and art, logic and imagination
6. Cultivation of grace and fitness
7. Recognition of interconnectedness of all things and phenomena [Systems thinking]

An emphasis on the teaching of higher-order thinking processes does not suggest the elimination of the importance of basic skills. Basic skills and creative teaching and learning are not polar opposites. Their mutualistic contribution to human development results from maintaining a balance between them. Recent government requirements for regular testing of reading and mathematics skills presents a challenge to teachers at all levels to maintain a balance between factual learning and the art of thinking, especially at the level of systems.

A plethora of resources for the teaching of creative and other higher-order thinking processes is readily available. Creative teachers do not depend upon ideas from resources, but rather cultivate the art of designing their own systemic thinking strategies that relate to the material being studied and to the nature and interests of their own particular class. E. Paul Torrance provides guidelines for the design of creative thinking activities at any age level (Torrance and Safter, 1990).

For teachers with an interest in adding the exercise of the environmental brain to the program, a few general recommendations are offered.

1. Design structured environmental encounters that lead to awareness and systems thinking.
2. Provide plenty of opportunities for students to think and be heard in an environment of trust between and among teacher and students.
3. Model and encourage standards of respect for individual differences.
4. Practice the search for commonalities of "opposites."
5. Practice and establish habits of mind mapping.
6. Concentrate on dialogue as opposed to debate in group discussion.
7. Provide reading materials and information on environment-based events and programs.
8. Encourage independent environmental study and group projects that result in community service.
9. Design thinking activities based on brainstorming and the principle of deferred judgment.
10. Display/design maps and charts of global environmental interrelatedness: sea, winds, air, temperature, rainfall. Investigate and discuss issues of global warming.
11. Follow newspaper reports of government environmental protection policy and issues.

David Orr, in *Earth in Mind: On Education, Environment, and the Human Prospect* (1994), offers strong words for educational leadership.

> The great ecological issues of our time have to do in one way or another with our failure to see things in their entirety. That failure occurs when minds are taught to think in boxes and not taught to transcend those boxes or to question overly much how they fit with other boxes. We educate lots of in-the-box thinkers who

perform within their various specialties rather like a dog kept in the yard by an electronic barrier. And there is a connection between knowledge organized in boxes, minds that stay in those boxes, and degraded ecologies and global imbalances. The situation is tragic in that many suspect where all of this is leading but believe themselves powerless to alter it.

CHAPTER 4

Notions Regarding Ideas
and Intellectual Leadership

There are two ways to slide easily through life: to believe everything or to doubt everything; both ways save us from thinking.

— *Alfred Korzybski*

THE PROVOCATIVE CHALLENGE of exploring the concepts of *ideas* and *intellectual leadership* is the dance between explosion and implosion of imagery and perception. Jean Charcot reminded us that "Theory does not prevent the facts from existing," and while I sorted through theory, I found myself driven by curiosities about the facts. However, the best I can do is to discuss the findings from reference works and literature, and offer some possible interpretations of connections between the concepts under investigation.

The art of creating new ideas provided the focus of the discipline of creativity since its inception when J. P. Guilford presented the American Psychological Association with his Model of the Structure of Intellect (Guilford, 1968). Strategies for stimulating and rewarding the production of new ideas for solving new problems have had international dissemination through the leadership of the Creative Education Foundation in Buffalo, New York. The search for understanding the creative force as a powerful component of the human brain/mind is not new in human history. Philosophers through the ages puzzled and speculated about the mysterious process that begets new ideas.

In a complex, dynamic society the issue of effective leadership takes on increasing dimensionality and demands higher quality thinking. Understanding the mental mechanism that produces creative ideas for meeting new challenges relates directly to quality thinking of effective leadership. This article explores two questions:

1. Where do ideas come from?
2. What does idea production have to do with leadership?

⑥

Defining *Ideas*

The safest path for approaching the subject is through the established authority of an unabridged dictionary. It becomes obvious that the defining of *idea* preoccupied the master thinkers throughout recorded history and, for all we know, long before that.

- Plato's definition was holographic and spoke of the "transcendent universal" and archetype, defined as "the original pattern or model of which all things of the same type are representations or copies." Jung's definition is an enhancement: "An inherited idea or mode of thoughts derived from the experience of the race and present in the unconscious of the individual."
- Locke related *ideas* to sensation or reflection.
- Aristotle interpreted *ideas* as a "form-giving cause," suggesting a process moving from abstract to concrete (from so-called "right-brain" inspiration to "left-brain" product).
- Berkeley introduced the notion of "percept" or "an impression of an object obtained by use of the senses."
- Hume limited his perception of *idea* to a representation of an association of memory in a closed system of self.
- Kant extended *idea* to a level of transcendentalism and nonempirical reason.
- Hegel assigned *idea* to the "highest category, the complete and final product of reason and its realization."

So the implications of early thinkers began to relate *idea* to a process transcendent, supersensible, and metaphysical, as well as intellectual, subtle, and paradoxical. *Idea* seems to be connected to metaphysics, scientific knowledge, and the origin and structure of space/time relationships of the universe. What is incomprehensible about this task is that we are trying to make *ideas* comprehensible.

By this time, the brain is reeling with the ambiguities and contraries and connections attendant on the definitions, and not getting any closer to facts. To further complicate things, attention must be paid to a number of terms so intimately related to *idea* that they cannot be ignored.

- *Intuition:* "To look at; to contemplate; coming to direct knowledge or certainty without reasoning or inferring; revelation by insight of innate knowledge; immediate apprehension or cognition; akin to instinct; direct insight to reality; quick leap into another's soul" (Webster's 1976). Collier's Encyclopedia extends *intuition* to include "immediate apprehension of truth," also "metaphysical and moral questions as reality, and bordering on religious mysticism."
- *Imagery:* As it figures into much of the discussion of *idea*, it is the "calling up of a mental picture, a product of imagination."
- *Imagination:* This concept can be described as a creation of the mind, especially the power to invent "the novel and the unreal by altering or combining the elements of reality" through the use of fantasy.
- *Insight:* The act of "apprehending the inner nature of things" or of seeing intuitively.

So it is quite clear that terminology associated with *idea* begins to doubleback on itself in a continuous interwoven system with "no clear-cut beginning and so far no dead end." A relevant article in *The Tarrytown Letter* (October 1983), recognized "The Three I's of Indian Education," namely, intuition, imagination, insight. It seems important to acknowledge the fact that the processes that take on so much relevance in the exploration of *idea* are present and, in many cases, more fully utilized in cultures other than the Western world, and become a mark of humanity rather than of levels of what is often referred to as "civilization."

⑥
Ideas and the Creative Processes

All of the aforementioned I-factors cluster around the notion of creativity in one way or another. All have something to do with the means by which original thoughts present themselves. In *The Act of Creation*, Arthur Koestler (1964) described the process of creativity as a "bisociation" of seemingly unrelated planes of thoughts, or a sudden meaningful connection that, in his words, "makes the mind turn a summersault" and bring spontaneous illumination and insight, whether it be in getting the joke, solving the problem, or having an intensely aesthetic experience. Koestler's theory of the creative process is in many quarters considered a seminal work in the discipline of creativity.

The creative production of an *idea* analyzed and researched by the specialized branch of educational psychology, can be identified by four cognitive factors of creativity: fluency, flexibility, originality, and elaboration. As early as 1965, while at the University of Minnesota, E. Paul Torrance designed tests for identification and measurement of these factors. In addition to the cognitive factors, a number of affective factors are recognized as contributing to the production of creative ideas: risk taking, independence, tolerance for ambiguity, preference for complexity, sense of humor, sensitivity, awareness. Recently the quality of altruism began appearing on the list of perceived qualities of the creative personality and hence likely to lead to new *ideas*.

⑥
The Lightbulb Experience

Cartoonists seem to agree that to communicate the sudden arrival of a new *idea* it is best indicated symbolically by drawing a lightbulb over the character's head. Such a symbol may be an improvement over the semantic method. The personal response to the recognition that a good new *idea* has been born can be one of "profound awe" such as one might feel when a sudden blaze of light penetrates the darkness.

"Looking into the dark in order to see" and finding sudden illumination in a new *idea* relates well to the archetypal lightbulb.

And what lights the light? The question of mental connections is basic. The interaction of manipulation of intellect and stored knowledge with creative processing determines the arrival and level of the creative product. In dictionary terms, *intellect* is defined as "the power of knowing rather than feeling or willing; a penetrating experience, getting at abstract substance." Passive intellect, *possible* intellect, and *potential* intellect were suggested as various forms. It is said that one cannot create in a vacuum, hence the argument for the accumulation of a vast storehouse of knowledge and experience. When the forces of that accumulation and of the creative urge, operating from cognitive and affective domains at full speed, act and interact upon one another, the procedures of preparation, illumination, and verification are brought to bear on the production of a creative thought.

Ideas may be innate, concrete, or abstract. They may come about as a result of the deliberate direction of intense energy (as in the processes of synectics and brainstorming) or they may come about unbidden during a period of relaxation or in a preconscious state. They may come by means of incubation when mental processes practice a kind of remote viewing and produce connections not available in the totally conscious state. Albert Einstein is quoted as saying that one will find that it is impossible to force oneself on the imagination, but that sometimes "when eating an apple, the idea will present itself and say, 'Here I am.'"

Authorities suggest that primary creativity, or major breakthroughs in the creative process have been the result of incubation, whereas secondary creativity, or the adapting and modifying type of *idea*, is likely to result from deliberate pressure to produce. In any case, in simple terms, creativity might be said to be "looking at one thing and seeing something else." The "something else" is supplied by the mind's eye with its awareness and insight into both micro and macro dimensions, separately and simultaneously, in their extreme polarities and in their capacities for balance.

It is possible that to bring about these encounters with the "intimate immensities" one may need to have available a generous supply of creativity, fantasy, feeling, experience, ability to play, humor, child-likeness (not childishness), even the ability to sleep and dream. In fact, the process may require "an ego that can leave the stage."

⑥

Leadership and Its Changing Patterns

The Institute of Public Affairs at the University of Minnesota under the direction of Harlan Cleveland instituted a program in Education for Reflective Leadership. Cleveland (1980) describes leadership as "physical energy, hard thinking, persuasive style, taste for ambiguity, unwarranted optimism, preference for motion [with history or against it]." Intellectual leadership, according to James McGregor Burns (1978), adds something more.

> A person concerned critically with values and purposes that transcend immediate practical needs; the person who deals with analytical ideas and data alone is a theorist; the one who works only with normative ideas is a moralist; the person who deals with both and unites them through disciplined imagination is an intellectual.

Two of the enduring examples of intellectual leadership are U Thant and Dag Hammarskold, both former secretaries general of the United Nations. The distinguishing quality of their leadership was the consistency of their behavior with the *ideas* they professed. Both retained a balance between action and solitude, and consistently modeled a global, spiritual behavior that stands as a model for intellectual leadership.

The seminal work of James McGregor Burns discussed intellectual leadership along with the concept of "Ideas as Moral Power" and referred to leadership of "large ideas, broad direction, and strong commitment" (Burns, 1978). He says of leadership:

1. Leadership is collective. One-person leadership is a contradiction in terms.

2. Leadership is causative. True leadership is not merely symbolic or ceremonial.
3. Leadership is morally purposeful, choosing key values and creating a social structure that embodies them.
4. Transforming leadership is elevating. It is moral but not moralistic. Leaders engage with followers, but from higher levels of morality; in the enmeshing of goals and values both leaders and followers are raised to more principled levels of judgment.

The development of the concept of transforming leadership as a new direction beyond transactional leadership is at the base of Burns's theory on leadership. He makes the following distinction between the two. Transactional leadership is based on leaders who approach followers with the purpose of exchanging one thing for another—jobs for votes, favor for favor or support, and so on. On the other hand, transforming leadership, toward which society is moving, helped along by communication that makes information universally accessible, creates a dynamic connection to the *ideas* of other enlightened, systemic thinkers and observers of the human scene.

> Transforming Leadership, while more complex, is more potent; the transforming leader recognizes and exploits an existing need or demand of a potential follower. But, beyond that the transforming leader looks for potential motives in followers, seeks to satisfy higher needs, and engages the full person of the follower. The result of transforming leadership is a relationship of mutual stimulation and elevation that converts followers into leaders and may convert leaders into moral agents. (Burns, 1978)

⑥
The Global Brain

Where do ideas come from? A search for answers can lead through ever greater complexities and cosmic possibilities. *The Global Brain*, a significant publication by Peter Russell (1983), speculates on "The Evolutionary Leap to Planetary Consciousness" and examines theoretical connections between individual consciousness and the fate of the planet. Where do ideas come from? If we asked Rupert Sheldrake, (1983), author of *A New Science of Life*, he would talk about his theory of "morphic resonance," which says that the brain acts partly as a "receptor or tuning device which tunes into a wide spectrum of species knowledge," and suggests "entirely new ways of seeing DNA, regeneration, the brain, memory, reincarnation, and creativity. Not to mention intuition." His theory suggests a whole new way of thinking about the brain after the manner of Jung's theory of the collective unconscious. It may be that humanity is on the brink of a major leap in the understanding of *ideas*, their origin and transmission. We may come to realize that "humanity is like some vast nervous system, a global brain, to which each of us contributes" (Russell, 1983).

⑥

Summary

Certainly we can agree that we are at a unique time in the history of understanding ourselves, our *ideas*, and our place in the holographic universe. Now that we have all seen photographs of "The Blue Pearl"—our earth—or what the astronaut Edgar Mitchell refers to as "The Little Blue Marble"—taken from the moon, we can for the first time perceive "spaceship earth," our home, in relation to the vast universe, and ourselves as participating in the interpretation of its mysteries. The opportunity is greater than ever for leadership in the discovery and communication of great *ideas* that will help the human family on toward its highest destiny.

CHAPTER 5

Creativity as a Catalyst for Integrative Thinking and Learning

Everyone has, simply by existing, a right to be intelligent, and to be provided with a way to become consistently more intelligent. This is a right that must be recognized and held sacred. Above all, the necessary conditions for the exercise of this right must be available. This is society's mission and the primary obligation of its leaders. All of them.

— Luis Alberto Machado, 1983

⑥

Evolution of a Discipline

FIFTY YEARS AGO J. P. Guilford introduced the concept of creative divergent thinking as an authentic factor in the structure of human intellect and opened the doors to the study and promotion of creativity. Since that time, interest in the understanding of the creative process and its application has grown. A discipline of creative studies has been developed and identifies four relevant specific issues for investigation and analysis: the creative person, the creative process, the creative product, and the creative press (climate for its expression). Countless research projects, books, and resources on creativity circulate in academic programs and throughout the general public. Workshops and seminars raise an awareness of the potential for creative thought and innovative action.

Early attention to creative imagination resulted in the establishment of the Creative Education Foundation in Buffalo, New York, which became an international resource center for creativity. The annual Creative Problem Solving Institute sponsored by the foundation attracts hundreds of participants from all over the world, producing a growing force of creativity leadership. Winslow Press, under the editorship of Morris Stein (2001) publishes annually a collection of essays by "Creativity's Global Correspondents," dedicated to the "strengthening of bonds between creativity teachers, researchers and trainers around the world through the dissemination of information rapidly and inexpensively." Creativity, then, becomes the instrument that influences integrative thinking, from local to international populations.

The teaching of creative thinking and problem solving directly enhances the development of individual creative potential. "We have arrived at a time in history when all higher order processes of thinking must be deliberately taught, and must take their place within the traditional curriculum with its emphasis on skills and content. Methods and materials are available for teaching the processes of creative thinking and critical thinking, as well as for evaluative thinking, systemic, visionary thinking, problem solving, and decision making" (Bleedorn, 1993). Strategies are also necessary to remove the barriers to creative productive thinking in groups.

The widespread popular use of the word *creativity* puts it in jeopardy of being applied superficially and with limited understanding or respect for the powerful significance of the creativity force. This usage endangers its meaning not only in individual human development and team building but beyond the inner circle of its application to the furthermost reaches of human experience. The creativity force is a human resource that applies to systems and transformations and on to the transition of all of society to a better world (Bleedorn, 1998).

⑥

Creative and Other Quality Thinking Processes

Creativity as a significant human force in a changing society leaps "out of the box" as a way to address the teaching of other quality thinking processes, including critical thinking; complex, integrative thinking; global awareness (not to be confused with globalization as applied to commerce); systemic thinking; futuristic thinking; and paradoxical thinking. The sensational evolution of technology, both hardware and software, strongly influences learning and development. Most children are well rehearsed in the value of computers for learning and stimulation. On the other hand, the maximum use of the human mind, that magical system of thought that is the birthright of every person, has been largely left to chance. Lester Milbrath (1996), in his book *Learning to Think Environmentally*, reminds us that most cultural influences condition us to think systematically, or linearly, in a straight, logical line. Now our complex, interrelated world requires that we think *systemically*, aware of all the interactive parts that make up the whole.

In contrast to thinking systematically, systemic thinkers

> focus on wholes rather than on parts. Within wholes they concern themselves with relationships more than objects, with process more than structures, with networks more than hierarchies. In a system, a given effect not only radiates through the system, it also feeds back and changes the factor that caused it. (Milbrath, 1996)

The complexity in the world and in most daily lives requires the capacity to think in terms of integrated parts and interactive systems. Educational experiences specifically need to recognize and cultivate systemic thinking up, down, and sideways across the levels of teaching and administration. To do less is to deny the responsibility of education to prepare students for realistic, meaningful participation in a democracy.

⑥

Freedom to Think and Be Heard

This discussion is not a recommendation to abandon traditional linear, systematic thinking altogether and replace it with systemic thinking. The integration of a full range of thinking processes is possible in classrooms as well as in boardrooms everywhere despite cultural con-ditioning and modeling of competitive, polarized habits of thought. The art of integrating two polarized diverse parts into a unified whole requires thinking at the level of paradox that, according to philosophers, is the highest form of intellect. Students at every level of intellect have the right to think and be heard within an open-ended structure of learning that encourages integration of subject matter and basic skills with personal experiences and belief systems.

Teachers need the freedom to teach according to standards of indi-vidual learning and thinking diversities. The human urge to grow and enhance oneself is best served when the system includes respect for in-dividual talents at the same time it develops excellence and accounta-bility. A teaching staff of dedicated teachers with an understanding of creative teaching principles and strategies could do much to solve problems of negative attitude and boredom in students (Torrance, 1995; Torrance & Safter, 1990).

Human nature is much too complex to be force-fitted into specific labels and categories. Perceiving students as individual complex systems in the continuing process of growth and evolution is a more re-alistic basis for the delivery of education. Labeling can be seriously dis-abling. Relying solely on measurable and countable factors of ability limits student assessment and development. Students are unique, complex systems rather than a collection of statistical data.

Master teachers understand the qualitative factor in education that transcends the traditional emphasis on quantitative data and standard-ization. Paul Wellstone, a U.S. senator, agrees with many educators who deplore the "overemphasized high-stakes standardized testing that is being touted as the new education reform" (Wellstone, 2001). An of-ficial focus on a single test as a measure of student achievement takes the excitement out of teaching and learning for both students and teachers. One alternative to standardized testing is receiving increased attention. "Educative assessment" is described as a self-assessment system that "provides students and teachers with feedback and oppor-tunities they can readily use to revise their performance on these or similar tasks" (Wiggins, 1998).

A reorganization of schooling could benefit by modeling the business trend of changing from officially designated management to a pattern of integrated leadership that includes the ideas and services of undesignated, untitled leadership within self-organizing systems. Including different levels of authority in school planning integrates a variety of perspectives in serving a diversity of students. Absolute dependence upon traditional exclusive administrative practices risks the exclusion of creative, qualitative factors such as flexibility, risk taking, and trust, which underscore greater individualizing of teaching.

⑥

Future Trends

A significant example of creative consideration of separate global issues is the annual conference of the World Future Society. The theme of the 2001 meeting in Minneapolis, Minnesota, was Future Scope 2001: Exploring the 21st Century. The issues explored in the program included business, creativity, economics, education, environment, government, health, international perspectives, religion, technology, and work/careers. Attention to the often polarized issues of technological and human values was well balanced. It provided an experience in the integration of different specializations, merging the separate parts into an effective whole.

When the World Future Society added the discipline of creativity to the official conference list of issues, they drew attention to the importance of creative thinking and learning, not only as a natural human force that contributes to human growth and development, but also as a catalyst for the future integration and collaboration of all the separate parts and pieces of society and its institutions. The conference's keynote speakers made direct reference to the educational argument for deliberate attention to the teaching of thinking processes, and reminded the audience that the human mind has to be considered the dominant force in today's world.

Harlan Cleveland (2001) made his annual contribution to the wisdom and vision of the conference's message in his presentation on

"The Nobody-in-Charge Society: Chaotic or Chaordic?" The prediction that organizations will move from hierarchical management to uncentralized patterns of operation requires a new kind of complex, integrative thinking. Schools concerned about their critical role in preparing a citizenry for meaningful participation in the human commons will be increasingly serious about the big question, "What shall we teach and how shall we teach it?" (See the discussion in chapter 2.)

U.N. Secretary General Kofi Annan, in a recent address, made a case for integrative thinking.

> Our enemy now is indifference. The belief is that there are many worlds, and the only one we need to care about is our own. That belief is false. There is one world, one humanity. And human security—genuine, equitable and lasting—is indivisible. (Annan, 2002)

⑥

Summary

Society is increasingly aware of the need for a major transition. We have changed everything we do except the way we think. Because almost every important thing we do depends on our habits of thought, we must change those habits to fit a complex, emerging global society. It is possible to specifically teach the understanding and application of creative, integrative habits of mind. The freedom to think at the highest possible level is an essential part of every human's intellectual growth and maybe the ultimate destiny of the human race.

CHAPTER 6

The Integration of Creative
and Critical Thinking

*If humanity is to pass safely through the present crisis on
earth, it will be because a majority of individuals are now
doing their own thinking.*

— Buckminster Fuller

THE NATURAL EVOLUTIONARY development of the art of thinking at
higher, more complex levels is joined in current times by the deliberate
study of processes of thinking, not only as separate and distinct classi-
fications but especially as integrated, interrelated, and interactive
systems. Dynamic, global changes in human affairs require creative and
critical thinking directed toward new, more complex thought patterns
and collective behavior.

The accumulation of more than 50 years of study concerned with
creative thinking and behavior is having increased application
throughout educational and business settings. Recent years have seen
a proliferation of attention to the study and application of critical
thinking in response to the diversity of human challenges. This
article is concerned with the proposition that the separate studies of
creative and critical thinking have a naturally integrative propen-
sity, and that what may be perceived as opposites or "contraries" have
the potential for productive mutuality. The paradoxical unity of differences in creative and critical thinking acknowledges not only the am-
bivalent, but also the harmonious qualities of these higher thinking
orders.

In *No Limits to Learning*, the authors Botkin, Elmandjera, and Malitza
(1979) added the global dimension to the expectation for unlimited
growth in the evolution of human thinking possibilities. The second

meeting of the International Club of Rome, as reported by Botkin and colleagues, argued that there are no limits to learning and that the "global mind" has unlimited potential to think, to grow, to evolve, and to respond positively to change. This optimistic outlook for a global mind change was in sharp contrast with the report of the first meeting of the International Club of Rome, which focused on threats to the planet of population explosion matched against the accelerating depletion of the earth's natural resources.

The study and application of creative and critical thinking in education, business, and throughout society provides a partial solution to the many challenges of change. Pioneers in early studies of creativity such as Torrance (1979), MacKinnon (1978), Getzels and Jackson (1962) and Guilford (1968) have been followed by current authorities like Amabile (1983), Sternberg (1988), and Gardner (1985) in creating a direction of study and inquiry that is attracting growing attention within the academic community. Isaksen and Murdock (1988) explored the development of the study of creativity and the general outlook for its emergence as a discipline, concluding that, not only in education but also in the fields of business and management, recognized needs and increasing practices exist for teaching creative, critical, and other higher-level thinking skills.

For many years the teaching of critical thinking in college philosophy courses was based on traditional studies of Aristotelian logic and deductive reasoning. Beginning with the work of Glaser (1941), studies of critical thinking were extended well beyond the classical concepts of critical analysis and logical, sequential thought. They have developed into a body of knowledge and recommended teaching activities designed for educational settings with the purpose of promoting responsible, fair-minded critical thinking and decision making. Although the history of their separate developments may cause creative and critical thinking to be perceived as separate and distinctive processes, their most effective applications are exemplars of highly integrated, dialectical thought.

Urgent arguments for the deliberate teaching of processes of both creative and critical thinking have centered around the reality of new complexities in the transition to a global society. The new age of global citizenship demands the fullest possible development of a global brain/mind, not only for its official leadership but throughout the world's populations. Bleedorn (1989) has argued that

> Freedom of thought, conscience and religion or belief is a right proclaimed in Article 18 of the Universal Declaration of Human Rights adopted by the United Nations General Assembly in 1948. It could be argued that the human right to think at higher, more complex levels and, accordingly, to behave at levels of mutuality, is a necessary added freedom if the reality of diversity in origin, culture, religion, and belief systems in the global family is to find harmony.

Harlan Cleveland, in his preface to *The Knowledge Executive* (1985), argued for an understanding of the ability of the human mind to entertain and integrate what William Blake called "the contraries."

> The human brain delights in the balance of contrasting thoughts. The most effective rhetoric often exploits an apparent paradox. Truth seems often to come wrapped in small, paradoxical packages. I have come to believe that the art of executive leadership is above all a taste for paradox, a talent for ambiguity, and the capacity to hold contradictory propositions comfortably in a mind that relishes complexity.

Absolute and conflicting beliefs are divisive. Thinking beyond polarities of differences to the level of paradox promotes understanding and reduces discord. It is suggested here that creative and critical thinking have equal importance in the transition to new and higher levels of thinking and learning, and that they are both important and necessary to each other in the systemic realities. The same higher levels of thinking that recognize commonalities and harmonize differences are prerequisite to peaceful, productive behavior in a diverse global society regardless of cultural or national origin.

Because of the diverse nature of the concepts and functions of creative and critical thinking, this article is intended for a readership reflective of a variety of perspectives concerned with the understanding and development of new ways of thinking individually and collectively. Events of the new century highlight the urgent need for changed patterns of thinking across the entire spectrum of global citizenry-teachers, learners, researchers, managers, and leadership of every kind. It is a sign of mental maturity to exhibit the systemic interactive nature of thought and behavior.

Richard Paul (1990) made a major contribution to the understanding and development of critical thinking and its legitimate place in the processes of learning. He made a distinction between "uncritical persons, critical persons, weak sense critical thinkers, and strong sense critical thinkers" (Paul, 1993). He elevated the concept of critical thinking well above its more traditional interpretations and argued for the enlightened perceptions that recognize the logic of processes of creative critical thinking and critical creative thinking. Paul made an early case for teaching critical thinking as an intellectual skill that enables one to decide rationally what to believe or do. He suggested that the practice of making the implicit explicit in arriving at reasonable judgments acknowledges factors below the level of conscious awareness in decision-making processes.

Application of the selective use of divergent and convergent thinking processes, similar to concepts of creative and critical thinking, is fundamental to the creative problem-solving process (Parnes, 1981). The principle of *deferred judgment* teaches separate but equal use of different modes of thinking, with the spontaneous freedom of divergent, creative thinking producing alternative ideas and the delayed convergent, evaluative process making choices and judgments. Critical thinking, in its more evolved nature, represents a trend toward the conceptualizing of a "unity of opposites" in contrast to more traditional, limiting perceptions of polarized categories and labels.

The concept of "making knowledge through disagreement" is central to the seminal work of David W. Johnson and Roger T. Johnson (1992) with their focus on cooperative learning. They promoted the practice of creative and critical thinking through controversy. Classroom practices in skills of empathic listening and flexible thinking are supported by conditions that contribute to constructive controversy and a synthesis of differences. The concept of productive thinking through the process of mind that makes unity of differences has application in learning experiences at all levels (Johnson & Johnson, R., 1992).

Theoretically based structures and procedures for directing a process that results in conflict resolution have social and political value at a time in history when cultural pluralism and global interrelatedness are adding to the need for transcending traditional, dualistic thinking practices. Cultivation of higher-level reasoning processes can overcome the factionalism and hostilities of single-minded biases. Creative and critical thinking help to remove the frames and boundaries of minds that are being called on for bold new initiatives in the transition to a global society.

Events in the political and human affairs of the "new world order" make an urgent demand not only on the thinking of designated leaders but on the thinking and perceptions of every member of the human family who shares responsibilities for leadership in a more undesignated role. Disturbing events and conditions in countries all around the world today leave no doubt that a transition from traditional to "transforming leadership" is a compelling need in the hope for a greater harmony of global differences. The power and purpose of human thought habits drive the kind of human behavior that defines a culture.

Things take time. An important book by Mikhail Gorbachev (1988) carried the title, *Perestroika: New Thinking for Our Country and the World.* It is unclear how much attention has been paid to the call for new thinking in the world since 1988. It seems clear enough that for much of the population the old habits of thought still prevail.

If creative and critical thinking have the potential to produce new and positive behaviors among people of difference who are learning to get along, the question arises, "Can it be taught?" Studies of new understandings and scenarios of new and expanded applications and resources testify to the fact that almost anyone can learn to develop his or her innate creative and critical thinking abilities. This article is intended to contribute to the extension and expansion of interest in the teaching of new ways of thinking and behaving appropriate to new global realities and visions of the future. The shift from an emphasis on separate parts and components to a more configurative perception of the "whole pattern" is inherent in the creative and critical thinking qualities that become more thoroughly teachable as they become better understood.

A quotation from Jonas Salk serves the argument.

> Therefore, it is in the best interest of the species, from an evolutionary point of view, for individuals with problem-solving attributes, as well as those possessing other creative and innovative traits, to be recognized. This requires an attitude and a system directed to the selection of those who would also serve the species' interest and not only the interest of the individual. The present serious human predicament requires all our creative energies for its resolution. (Salk, 1983)

This chapter is reprinted with permission from *American Behavioral Scientist*, 27, no. 1 (September–October 1993), pp. 10–20.

CHAPTER 7

Humor and the Creative Intellect

A merry heart doeth good like medicine but a depressed spirit drieth the bones.

— *Proverbs 17:22*

THIS DISCUSSION IS one of humor. Contrary to most expectations, its purpose is not to provoke laughter, but to make a case for laughter as a serious business. Few people know anything about humor—what laughter is, why it is, what a sense of humor is all about and how to cultivate it, what a joke is, and why it is a joke. Humor is one of the least understood and investigated of human emotions. Today, signs show that humor is coming into focus as a viable and critical direction of study that enhances our understanding of human behavior and levels of thought.

⑥

Humor and Creativity

From the beginning, studies of the creative personality listed characteristics of the creatively talented, which invariably included the quality of a sense of humor (Torrance, 1962; Gowan, 1968). For example, the identification of giftedness in children depends to a considerable degree upon observations of classroom behavior as a means of recognizing creative quality thinking (Torrance, 1979; Renzulli, 1976). Providing opportunities and a supportive climate for the expression of humor in the classroom at any level presents a challenge for teachers concerned with a broad concept of intellectual strength.

The mental processes of humor and creativity are inseparable. An appropriate place to begin the understanding is with the landmark work, *The Act of Creation* (Koestler, 1964). Koestler's introductory section, titled, "The Jester," describes the relationships between creativity and laughter. Humor, then, as represented by means of his theory of bisociation, can be perceived as one of three distinct but interrelated processes: what makes us laugh; what helps us to understand; what causes us to wonder. In simple terms, bisociation is described as a process of the mind where two heretofore unrelated ideas or planes of thought are suddenly brought together in a recognized relationship requiring a special kind of mental agility or cognitive "acrobatics." Both the creation of a subtle joke and the recreative act of "getting the joke" require a mental operation on more than one plane (bisociation), rather than on a single plane (association). The subtlety and complexity of bisociative thinking, as in the logical structure and emotional dynamics of humor, offer stimulating processes for quality thinkers of any age.

Koestler presents his ideas in the form of a Triptych showing the relationships between humor (the *ha-ha* experience), discovery (the *ah-ha* experience), and the poetic image or art (the *ahhhhhh* experience), flowing from the self-assertive to the self-transcending mode in figure 7.1 (Koestler, 1964).

Figure 7.1 • Bisociation: Humor and the Creative Process

The Triptych

Humor	Discovery	Art
Ha-Ha	**Ah-Ha**	**Ahhhhh**
Cosmic simile	Hidden analogy	Poetic image
Witticism	Epigram	Trouvaille
Satire	Social analysis	Allegory
Impersonation	Empathy	Illusion
Caricature	Schematization	Stylization
Pun	Word puzzle	Rhyme
Riddle	Problem	Allusion
Debunking	Discovering	Revealing
Coincidence	Trigger	Fate
Aggressive	**Neutral**	**Aesthetic**
Bathos		Pathos

Source: Arthur Koestler, *The Act of Creation* (New York: Dell Publishing, 1964).

๑
Programming Humor

The importance assigned to a sense of humor as an observable in-
dicator of quality thinking requires that more than an incidental,
cursory attention to humor be programmed into classroom and social
experiences. In our efforts toward achievement and our preoccupation
with records, paperwork, standardized tests, and competitive grading,
we may neglect the opportunity provided by periods of time specifically
designed for playfulness and laughter. A climate that encourages spontaneous, unprogrammed humor is as significant as the process of
schooling for scholars. The traditional lack of reward or positive re-
inforcement discourages talents in comic production from surfacing.
The practicing or potential comedian or comedienne is too often stifled
and perceived as a disrupter of classroom set procedures.

๑
Looking at Laughter

Arguments for the deliberate attention to creativity and humor are
based on a number of assumptions.

- Laughter is a natural and necessary process for all of humankind. It
  can modify differences, release tensions, and neutralize anxieties;
  the universal language of laughter fosters fellowship.
- Laughter enhances learning and well-being. A relaxed mind is inclined
  to be a receptive mind. Laughter is good medicine (Cousins, 1979).
- One's sense of humor is an important mark of one's personal
  identity. Quality thinkers are entitled to the satisfaction of laughing
  with others who share their style and level of humor.
- The level of humor relates to one's cognitive level. If a situation or
  joke is too simple, the complex thinker is not amused. Laughter is
  produced by the momentary puzzlement and the release of tension
  when the resolution presents itself. The thinker's mind must be
  challenged. Complex thinkers require complex challenges if they are
  to become seriously involved.

- A broad base of knowledge contributes to a broad-based sense of humor. Without a familiarity with the terms of information needed to interpret the "funny business," the listener misses the joke. Humor is a challenging and satisfying vehicle for thinkers who have gathered and stored a wide range of information.

- Emotional climate determines whether one laughs or laments. Teachers, parents, and other authority figures are climate-makers. Casual, supportive attitudes by role models can set free the spirit of fun in the external climate. The internal climate or personal affect at a given period is equally significant to a response to humor.

- The spirit of fun and playfulness is a vital ingredient in the self-actualizing process in Maslow's original hierarchy of needs (Maslow, 1973).

Humor relates directly to the practice of promoting right-brain simultaneous thinking (Ornstein, 1968). For example, creative humor in programming contributes to hemispheric balance. According to Howard Gardner (1981), the two hemispheres of the brain must work together in a whole-brain operation to appreciate the meaning of a metaphor and the punch line of a joke.

The process of humor and what it means to one's individuality are worthy of discussion and study both within and outside of a classroom. The privilege and power of laughter is too important to be left to chance.

⑥
Invitation to Variety in Forms of Humor in the Classroom

Because of the variety of forms of humor, plans for classroom activities need to studiously cover a number of content areas as identified in the Guilford Model of the Structure of Intellect (Guilford, 1977). The inclination to limit humor to its more familiar verbal forms would miss talents for humor expressed in symbols, in figural forms (visual and auditory), and in behaviors. With that reminder of the theoretical connection, let us proceed to a few examples of ideas for classroom use according to the forms of humor listed in Koestler's Triptych described earlier. Observing both the production of humor and the response to humor by students during planned thinking activities provides teachers with clues to high-level cognitive connections and creative thinking talents.

- *Comic simile:* Invite students to write original similes based on imagery or words specifically assigned from content of lessons or by personal choice. (Example: As quiet as a mouse backing into a pussywillow.) Note also the use of simile in exercises of sentence completion. (He was as nervous as . . . *or* She was moving faster than . . .) Clever responses can signal a special kind of thinking.
- *Witticism:* Clowning and wisecracks indicate talents in spontaneous humor not readily preprogrammed. As disconcerting and sometimes disruptive as they may be to carefully programmed procedures, the laughter produced by good-natured witticism and clever clowning and mimicry can also contribute to receptivity for learning. Researchers tell us that creatively talented students are inclined to use the "production of fantasy, incongruities, and absurdities to maintain an optimally varied and interesting environment" (McGhee, 1979). Creative minds produce their own variety when it is absent in school programs.
- *Satire:* Cartoons provide options for visual thinkers to communicate ideas. Use cartoons attacking political and social pretense to discuss the powerful statements possible in graphics. Collect cartoons without captions to practice understanding without the use of words or collect cartoons with captions, remove the captions and exchange them with others for the writing of original captions.The subtlety of the responses can reflect the complexity of thought.
- *Impersonation:* Discuss the art of impersonation, using familiar examples from the entertainment field. Have students watch the moves and styles of television personalities to mimic and present to the class for identification. In another exercise, one member of a team reads a description of a person or event and the other member

interprets by movement and exaggerated facial expressions the content of the reading.

- *Caricature:* Discuss the technique of exaggeration in drawings as a means of identification. Look at caricatures of famous people. Discuss distinguishing features and have students draw a caricature of themselves. Have them find a picture of favorite sports or entertainment hero or heroine and use it as a base for an original caricature of the person. Discuss the aggressive quality of some caricatures and of some humor. Discuss the use of humor as a "weapon."
- *Coincidence:* The laughter that follows actual or filmed action where two or more forces meet suddenly and unexpectedly in an accidental happening is a response to coincidence. Tensions of expectation can be dispelled in laughter. Watching comedy cartoons like *The Pink Panther* or some of the old-time movies provides many examples for rating the relative funniness of coincidental events.

⑥

Summary

A fundamental factor in a formula for the recognition and development of creative talents in humor is a relaxed, receptive, responsive, and alert attitude on the part of the teacher. Some knowledge of thinking styles and of developmental levels of humor helps to distinguish between intended and unintended naïve humor. A child's innocent, unwitting production of amusement for adults is not part of the intention of these observations. The emphasis must be on original spontaneous mental bisociations for "funny business" as opposed to the tiresome repetition of a funny line or the forced, artificial laughter that follows the trite and familiar or the example of other laughers.

As is the case with most efforts to analyze and classify the complexities of human behavior, specifics and absolutes won't do the total job. Sensitivity, intuition, and empathy are equally important to a sense of humor. The world is in serious need of laughter and good humor. Learning need not be grim. Business need not be humorless. The growth of the human family toward a mutualistic level of development may depend upon the ability of diverse cultures to laugh together. Humor may turn out to be one of the greatest unifying features of the human condition in the global village. Its deliberate recognition and encouragement early on and throughout society are vitally important and long overdue.

CHAPTER 8

In and Out of the Creativity Box

In collaboration with Frank Maraviglia

There is a tide in the affairs of men
Which, taken at the flood, leads on to fortune;
Omitted, all the voyage of their life
is bound in shallows and in miseries.
On such a full sea are we now afloat
And we must take the current when it serves
Or lose our ventures.

— Shakespeare

CERTAINLY THIS CHAOTIC transitional time in human history opens up numerous opportunities for the advancement of creativity everywhere. Radical change in the entire spectrum of human affairs focuses unprecedented attention politically and socially to issues of educational reform. Because functional democratic societies depend upon the participation of all of their citizens, futurists call for educational programs that prepare students for this new kind of world and new kinds of thinking. Education must realize its responsibility to provide educational experiences at every level of learning that will result in creative and other quality thinking processes.

Over the past 50 years of its development, the teaching of creative thinking focused on strategies for the development of individual creative potential, the skills of creative problem solving, analysis and research, grass roots leadership, and having fun in the process of creative thinking. Now the world is ready for a grand leap out of the creativity box. Without abandoning the focus on individual and group creativity training, now is the strategic time to promote the focus on creativity as an omnipresent force with universal dimensions. It offers a potential for dynamic service to a world and its institutions that face years of chaotic change and evolutionary development. It is time to add a global, futuristic factor to programs for personal challenge. It is time to motivate the world and its institutions to make better use of the natural human force for creative expression and growth present in almost everyone. To fail to do so seriously wastes the infinite resource and potential of the human mind.

The ideas addressed here present the combined thinking of two veterans in the practice of educational leadership in the discipline of creativity and creative problem solving and together offer seventy years of involvement with the Creative Education Foundation and its Creative Problem Solving Institute in Buffalo, New York. Most of those years were spent as leaders and colleagues of the Institute. Their interests in and dedication to the creativity discipline as educators give them a perspective described by Harlan Cleveland as "reflective practitioners and practical academics," which balances the "why" of theoretical philosophy with the practice of direct, purposeful experience. This writing attempts to provide a connecting piece for others interested in the significance of the current political and social zeitgeist as it relates to creativity and visionary leadership.

⑥

The Argument

The discipline of creativity evolved around the understanding and application of the Four Ps—the creative person, the creative process, the creative product, and the creative press (climate). A great deal has been accomplished in both educational and business settings for bringing about an increased awareness and practice of creative thinking and problem solving. Course content in university offerings, conference programs, popular literature, and business training seminars continue to make creativity a familiar theme worldwide. Such widespread popular use of the term *creativity* creates an assumption that the creative process is characterized only by its playful component within individual and group development. That assumption tends to limit efforts to establish a more official academic status to the discipline and to advance a broader view of creativity as a universal force present to a degree in everyone and seriously wasted in hierarchical organizations governed by leadership of exclusivity.

George Land's theory of transformation (Land, 1992) advances a relevant argument. In the first (formative) phase, any living system determines the pattern and form for accomplishing its purpose. In the second (normative) phase, the established pattern of operation is repeated and intensified. Conforming to the established norm is the standard modus operandi. The third (integrative) phase is characterized by a breakpoint period when the original purpose of the system is reviewed and its operation opened and expanded to include broadened, current perspectives. In a discussion of Land's work, Cliff Havener referred to the formative phase as the "Celebration of Creativity," the normative phase as the "Persecution of Creativity," and the integrative phase as the "Resurrection of Creativity" (Havener, 1999). The beginning of this new millennium offers the opportunity to express the importance of creative education, based on the needs of a global society in transition, to politicians and all of society with a reasonable expectation of receiving their attention.

The present complexities of society quite unknown 50 years ago when creativity and problem solving came onto the scene make it the right time for serious attention to the integrative phase of creativity. A breakthrough to new perspectives and creativity frontiers could combine in a bifurcation bump with the original and familiar creativity focus, and offer a rare opportunity to contribute to the overdue reform of higher education and other levels of learning.

The stakes for the business community are high; it depends on the quality of thinking that graduates of business programs bring to the workplace in the intensely competitive climate of global commerce. Management experts point out the need for more inclusive leadership from designated leaders. Exclusivity in management deprives the corporation of the contribution of its most creative employees. Undesignated leaders with advanced thinking and a perceptive sense of the dynamic system and its future possibilities can be silenced and lost if designated leaders are too exclusive in their style. Creative leadership means leadership not only in the teaching of creativity but beyond that to the practice of transforming leadership through creative thinking and behavior.

The critical nature of the times requires the voice and energy of perceptive minds, whether officially certified and properly labeled or not. In fact, minds that evolved independent of formal education by way of electronically available information—and its creative processing to a level of wisdom, systems, and a sense of the future common good— need to be guaranteed the right to think and be heard.

William Blake gave us an understanding of levels of perception that characterize the kinds of thinking so crucial for the present world in transition. Blake suggested that the opening of the "doors of perception" begins with a sensory awareness in which relevant information is absorbed through sight, sound, taste, smell, and all the other human senses. When that initial opening of the door of perception is expanded, the sensory information then moves to the abstract level that names and identifies, describes and communicates the perceptions. The next level further opens the doors to include the imaginative perceptions beyond the recognized realities. The fourth and near final level of perception visualizes the system and the possible future of all the observable trends. Beyond that structure Blake perceived the limitless, mysterious level of perception that he called "megatruth," or what could be known as higher consciousness or the superconscious mind (Ackroyd, 1995).

The teaching of creative thinking and problem solving in an integrated phase recognizes the social and political system and the art of thinking "beyond our region and beyond our time." The "bifurcation bump" of the creativity discipline includes the familiar objectives of personal and group creative development, and at the same time gives equal attention to visionary and integrative dimensions of the creativity force and its unlimited capacity for awareness of the interactive global system. Concern for global environmental preservation and the hope for a better quality of life for more of the earth's people depend upon creative and other higher-order thinking patterns the world over.

J. P. Guilford, in his comprehensive three-dimensional model of the structure of intellect, offered an understanding of the various capacities of the human intellect. His model demonstrates 150 ways of being smart. The six products of thinking in his model are listed in hierarchical order from the simplest to the most complex. Starting with thinking in single units, the list moves up through thinking in classes, in relationships, in transformations, in systems, and finally to the combination of all levels, which leads to implications that parallel Blake's level of visionary thinking (Guilford, 1977).

⑥

Out of the Creative Education Box

Agreement that the natural creativity force in most humans is a critical resource for positive change in the global future and that, in many cases, it has been blocked and silenced by traditional standardized education and closed cultural systems gives rise to certain questions: "How can the discipline of creativity contribute to the reform of education as a center of learning for informed and involved global citizenship?" and "What can proponents of creativity do to move creative studies to an academically recognized place of authority and authentic application at a time when political and public attention to education is at an all time high?"

We can begin by agreeing that the institutions of learning must move out of the box of standardization and the absolutism of labels based on quantitative measurement. With no factoring in of qualitative features of mind and personhood in the delivery of education, the cultivation of a concept of personal identity and significance is easily lost and along with it a base of self-confidence critical to effective learning and achievement.

Because higher education represents the ultimate in formal learning and certification, leadership for the trek "out of the creative education box" needs a strong, forceful presence in colleges and universities. It requires an awareness among power and administrative centers of the academically rigorous nature of authentic courses in creative thinking and problem solving. A major challenge is the task of overcoming the roadblocks set up by the "powers that be" when they make judgments about creative education based on assumptions that creative studies relates only to the arts or that all other programs have greater priority.

Perceptions need to move beyond the opinion that creativity studies in colleges and universities are intellectually lightweight and expendable. Studies in creativity taught creatively from an academic base of knowledge and understanding can be at least as demanding of academic standards as other courses and, in addition, can serve as a vehicle for the long overdue integration of learning and thinking. One of the highest priorities of education must be to create a population of world citizens capable of creative, complex, critical, systemic, visionary, global thinking. Public pressure for changes in higher education needs to be brought to bear in administrative circles where the specific teaching of quality thinking is seen as a responsibility of centers of advanced learning (Mestenhauser & Ellingboe, 1998). The service of academically qualified, certified, titled public figures ought to reflect a capacity for global, futuristic, visionary thought and judgment.

The discipline of creativity can contribute to the reform of education as a center of learning for informed and involved global citizenship by asserting the belief that all humans are from the beginning and by their nature motivated to learn and grow and enhance themselves. University students who are given a place for the acquiring of basic skills and knowledge, the freedom to think, the encouragement to express their creative ideas, and the support of significant specialists in a chosen field demonstrate a pattern of growth and development that will serve them in a lifetime of change and challenge.

From a practical point of view, German artist and philosopher Joseph Beuys believed creativity to be the "new currency for the transformation of society" (Beuys, 1998). The major international authority on creativity, E. Paul Torrance (Millar, 1995) has been reminding educators for years that the kinds of intelligence needed now differ from those needed a few years ago. In the same way, the kind of intelligence needed in the future will no doubt be different from what is needed today. More student-oriented integrative programming and more global awareness and vision on the part of university leadership could fulfill this predictive wisdom of such expert opinions.

Fifty years of study and research in the discipline of creativity produced a vast collection of teachers, trainers, and scholars who pioneered the movement to bring about the specific teaching of creativity and creative problem solving worldwide. The Creative Education Foundation in Buffalo, New York, functions as a networking center for effective leadership in introducing the study and practice of creative thinking and problem solving in schools at both K–12 and university levels. The limited progress in many cases results from entrenched, archaic organizational systems and firmly boxed-in habits of mind.

Now a new awareness, publicly expressed, sees the failure of educational systems in the world to produce graduates who can think at a level demanded by the dynamics and challenges of new global realities. Serious issues of world peace, environmental sustainability, quality of life for the expanding world population, regulation of world economy, and much more demand leadership and followership with thinking capacities equal to the task. Now, also, for the first time the issue of educational reform joins the usual list of political debates and candidate platforms. More and more citizens add their voices to the discussion. Political solutions expressed so far are limited to ideas like smaller class size and more money for teachers. Those with an inside view of institutions of learning can testify to the fact that changing the measurable and countable numbers is not enough to reform the system. Serious attention must focus on what is being taught as well as the nature and preparation of those teaching it. Predictions of the staggering number of new recruits needed for the teaching profession present both a challenge and an opportunity for new directions.

Politicians with educational reform on their minds and in their platforms need to be reminded of world changes that are driving the urgency for new designs of formal education. Especially the traditional system of higher education with its tightly structured programs and inflexibly categorized departments is overdue for change. A system that recognizes and encourages the integration of learning and thinking and that actually requires courses on creative and other higher order thinking processes would be a logical addition to the stated purposes of higher education—producing graduates who are not only ready for a career and competition in the market place, but are also ready to serve the common good and to participate meaningfully as concerned and informed global citizens.

❦

Creative Change Agents

Now is the time for proponents of creative education to capitalize on the public demand for educational reform all the way from kindergarten through higher education and beyond to lifetime learning and a speeded-up evolution of human thinking processes. Teachers and trainers, researchers and writers in the creativity field can move beyond individual-based analyses and strategies and on to influencing institutions of all kinds, including government. They can draw attention to the crisis in education and the critical role of creativity in dealing with the challenges of change. Both print and electronic media provide information that can serve as a current resource in arguments for the integration of higher order thinking throughout society. Political leadership all over the world needs and, in some cases, is ready for a new awareness of the kind of education crucial to a fully functioning democracy.

Some legislators express serious interest in solutions to problems of education. They are listening as never before to dedicated practitioners in education. The hope is that they are hearing from teachers who have moved out of the box of education-as-usual and who have a sense of the global system. One particular challenge is the realization of the immediate need in the country for thousands of new candidates for teacher education. That fact highlights the responsibility of centers for teacher training to include required courses in the philosophy and practice of processing the information overload in order to make new connections, find solutions for problems that previously never existed, and make judgments based on perceptions of a global interactive system.

Recruiting teacher candidates takes on importance as never before if incoming teachers are to help lead the way for new patterns of learning. Criteria for their selection must go far beyond the standard resume and include some indication of a creative spirit with a genuine passion for teaching and a commitment to remain for an extended time in the work of teaching. Effective teaching benefits from the modeling by the teacher and administration of qualities associated with creativity, such as flexibility, imagination, an orientation to systems thinking, resilience, risk taking, a tolerance for ambiguity, and a positive attitude, just to name a few.

The present situation offers educational and governmental in-stitutions good reason to listen seriously to the messages E. Paul Torrance and others have been sending to teachers for many years (Torrance, 1995). Educators in many parts of the world use the Torrance Tests of Creative Thinking to identify creative thinking talent and potential. His many publications provide teachers with under-standing and classroom strategies for identifying and cultivating creative thought in children and youth. His Incubation Model of Teaching (Torrance & Safter, 1990) fosters master teachers at every level who understand and practice the art of teaching basic skills of reading and mathematics through the use of creative learning and thinking strategies. The appearance of charter schools separate from total state jurisdiction underscores a trend in the direction of learning through the inclusion of direct purposeful experiences as advocated by the Torrance model.

High school graduates entering college after participating in experi-ential learning activities that enriched their learning and thinking will find the traditional college classes that demand passive learning and a focus on required "right answers" to be an interruption to their moti-vation for learning. Highly creative thinkers with an aptitude for inde-pendent thinking and discovery exhibit low levels of tolerance for au-thoritarian teaching methods and piecemeal bureaucratic curricular programming. Dropout rates among college students can be expected to include bright, creative thinkers with an appetite for learning that is poorly served in many traditional courses. The need for reform of education seems undisputed. The argument for more creative curricula needs to be included in the solution.

◈

Summary

Anyone serious about changes in education or any other institution would do well to remember that "every important thing we do depends on our habits of mind" (Ruggiero, 1988). Our culture, for many years, paid more attention to the urge to possess than to the urge to know. Concern for physical, economic, and cosmetic standards outpaced a balanced concern for our mental machinery and its natural urge to evolve and be exercised. For 12 years every person is required by law to attend school. Formal education beyond the legislated 12 years is an option chosen by many, especially those seeking preferred careers. Anyone with an awareness of the interactive nature of the changing global community can agree that somewhere within those years the specific processes and potentials of the human mind need to be addressed if we expect the world and its population to survive with a reasonable quality of life. Research in cognitive development and human differences in learning and thinking styles provide educational practitioners with information that supports greater attention to the teaching of creative, critical, and other higher order thinking.

Colleges and universities employ numerous teachers of creativity and problem solving who teach a number of courses related to cognitive development and quality thinking, including principles of the discipline of creativity. In many cases courses in creative thinking are combined with more traditional content in order to secure the approval of the curriculum committee. Most administrators in education as well as in the work place and in other institutions and organizations lack a background in the 50 years of academic development in creativity. They find little reason to support programs and to lend official approval to a place for creativity in academia. Because the traditional way of doing things is so closely related to the issue of control, the people who could initiate change are often the very ones whose control is threatened by new ideas.

Proponents of creativity need to be more vocal and aggressive in the promotion of creative studies during this time of political awareness and activity aimed at reform of education. They need to add to the urge for their own development and service to organizations the broader argument for challenging the world and its institutions to create a population of quality thinkers. They need to risk opening new doors for the inclusion of thinkers who see things differently and who can add the searchlight perspective of systems to the spotlight of individual focus.

Creative thinking and problem-solving input often find support among advocates of educational reform who are looking for ways to improve the status and quality of the teaching profession. The challenge remains for new kinds of training programs for the many new teachers required in the immediate educational future.

Communication with candidates for office, local and national, can create publicity and a place on meeting agendas for discussions of creativity in the classroom. Spokespersons in local meetings of concerned citizens and campaign promotions can create awareness in the community of the value of creative teaching of basic skills. The first step in change is awareness. After that step comes knowledge and finally wisdom in the evolution of human thought. With wisdom comes the reflection of basic human values like goodwill, a sense of community, trust, mutual respect, and responsibility.

Two recent publications argue for reforming the higher education curriculum (Mestenhauser & Ellingboe, 1998; Bleedorn, 1998). The one all-encompassing focus of reform perhaps should be the study of the earth as our home and the urgent need for everyone to understand its vulnerability and methods for its sustainability. At a minimum, every student at every level including university and college should have the privilege of environmental studies, and no one should graduate from college without it.

Creative thinkers and activists play a critical role in speeding up efforts toward positive change and growth in humans and their institutions. As far back as 1979 a report to the International Club of Rome by Botkin, Elmandjra, and Malitza discussed, "No Limits to Learning: Bridging the Human Gap." Schools need to better deliver the message, which still applies. The message, that human beings have a wealth of untapped resources of vision and creativity as well as moral energies with which to "bail humankind out of its predicament," must continue to be communicated (Botkin et al., 1979). People with this new learning perspective need to be mobilized. It is everyone's problem. It is everyone's leadership opportunity.

CHAPTER 9

Beyond the Creativity Frontier:
More Quality Thinking

*Thinking is an art with its own purposes, standards, prin-
ciples, rules, strategies, and precautions. And it is an art well
worth learning, for every important thing we do is affected by
our habits of mind.*

— *Vincent Ruggiero*

FIFTY YEARS AGO J. P. Guilford presented to the American Psychological
Association his Model of the Structure of Intellect. With that moment
he opened the floodgates of investigation and understanding of the
human creativity force and its value to personal development. For fifty
years, led by an assortment of dedicated scholars and educational entrepreneurs, the theories and practices of creative studies gradually
worked their way into university curricula and classrooms everywhere.
At the same time creative leadership in the public sector offers training
in the art of creative thinking and innovative action across the entire
spectrum of human activity.

Since the beginning, the center of information, research, and resources for the teaching of creative thinking and problem solving has
been the Creative Education Foundation in Buffalo, New York. The
Annual Creative Problem Solving Institute, sponsored by the Foundation, provides a gathering place for leadership in the development of
creativity studies nationally and, in more recent years, internationally
as an academic discipline.

Where the original focus centered on the development and teaching of
personal creativity and its expression, the scope of the discipline continues
to broaden to include other higher-order thinking processes. A partial list
of these quality thinking processes would include transformational

thinking, global awareness, systemic thinking, recognizing relationships, visionary futuristic thinking, intuitive and paradoxical thought, and critical thinking as defined in recent studies (Paul, 1990). The complex, dynamic nature of the times demands new kinds of thinking and problem solving everywhere that the world's people are trying to cope with monumental change and create a new, more just and peaceful society.

ⓖ
Guilford Revisited

It seems important now to look again at the fundamental theory of intellectual strengths and individual differences developed by J. P. Guilford 50 years ago. Not only did his work begin the development of the discipline of creative studies, but it also presented a construct for teaching the full range of thinking capacities. The products dimension on his Model of the Structure of Intellect (Guilford, 1977) is the only one arranged in a hierarchy, beginning with the least complex. The order begins with single units of thought and moves upward through relationships, transformations, systems, and finally implications, which includes the capacity to visualize and to entertain ideas with a time reality in the future. Thought products of units and classes are placed at the lower end of complexity. Recognizing relationships, thinking in systems, creating transformations, and visualizing the future implications of present realities are high-end products.

When the World Future Society included creativity, the arts, and new thinking in its listing of sociosphere issues at its World Future Society Conference a few years ago, the discipline of creative studies gained additional status as a factor to be addressed in the shared effort to create a better future for the earth's people. The natural evolution of the brain/mind to higher, more complex thought processes needs help when technological developments outpace philosophical growth. That help is available right now in the specific teaching of creativity and other high-end thinking processes in educational programs at all levels. Can we seize the moment and integrate the specific teaching of quality thinking with an educational reform package?

☙
Quality Thinking

Certainly in the United States, and perhaps in other places in the world, public attention to education is growing. At no previous point in time has so much political and public concern been directed at education, nor a time when the need for quality thinking was greater. So far, public recommendations for reform by candidates and public officials build mostly on traditional educational programs. Agendas for changes in education seem almost consistently to be limited to countable and measurable factors: higher salaries for teachers, smaller class sizes, greater student and teacher accountability by means of standardized basic skills tests, educational uses of technology, and expansion of preschool programs.

In addition to this focus on traditional basic skills and organizational structure, however, learners of all ages show a bottom-line need to engage in educational programs that discover and develop their capacity for creative and other quality thinking habits. All of us will spend the rest of our lives in a dynamic global society engaged in radical change and dependent for its survival as a functioning democracy on the wisdom and judgment and thoughtful participation of all of its citizens.

Courses in creative studies provide the cornerstone for the issue of quality thinking everywhere—in the corporate workplace, in the laboratory, in centers of government and human service, and wherever people gather to share their individual specialties for the common good. A society and its political leadership serious about educational reform will "get out of the box" of curricula as usual and make room for the specific teaching of high-end thinking processes.

☙
Creative Leadership for a Global Future

This enthusiastic response of students and general public to classes in creative studies could be the start of something even bigger. If the development of personal creativity could ripple out to include quality thinking in groups and teams with a shared purpose, a great deal of conflict and polarization could be avoided. Beyond group applications, the creativity effect would influence institutions and even reach into the greater interdependent international community. The key to changes in the quality of thinking would be the quality of leadership created during the schooling experience.

A study of the perceived current educational practices and the development of creative leadership for a global future found that there was no positive correlation (Bleedorn, 1988). Those findings may indicate that the current difficulty of moving from hierarchical, exclusive management styles to inclusive, creative leadership in business and other institutions could be mediated with the teaching of creative and other quality thinking. It may also be safe to assume that a similar study conducted today would produce more encouraging results.

Scholars and practitioners of creativity across the world are engaged, not only in the identification and development of creative potential in individuals of all ages, but also in the development of quality thinking wherever people gather in the mutual effort meet the demands of rapid and radical change, to bring about a unity of differences, to improve the quality of life for more of the earth's people, and to maintain the quality of their planetary home.

❦

A Daunting Task

At times during the 50 years of development of creativity and its teaching, progress seemed slow and laborious. Recent times show that the tireless efforts of the committed leaders are paying off. Creativity is coming to be recognized as a legitimate academic discipline. Creativity in the public sector is coming to be understood as a serious positive force in human activities (Bleedorn, 1998). In the corporate world creativity and innovation are readily recognized in the claim that "creativity equals capital" (Beuys, 1990). A growing trend indicates that effective leaders are building on the bedrock of creativity and expanding the daunting task of changing long-established habits of thought to include more high-capability thinking patterns.

The good news is that although many of the natural resources of earth are finite, the capacity of the human mind to change and grow is unlimited (Botkin et al., 1979). Technology moved the traditional focus of education from memory storage to the cultivation of talents for processing the overwhelming supply of available data in ways compatible with the systemic reality of the complex world. Electronic communication systems can make any concerned and enlightened thinker a potential player in the leadership campaign for new ways of thinking together.

⑥

Summary

At this transition time in human history when political and social forces are focused on necessary change in education, plans for reform will be incomplete unless they include the deliberate teaching of creative and other more advanced ways of thinking. Quality thinking for all citizens would help to move the world in new directions that perceive the world as it truly is—a shared, vulnerable earth at risk and a population capable of thinking patterns dedicated to its preservation and the preservation of a peaceful life for its people.

Some of the greatest thinkers have been trying to give us the big message for years. It is time for all educators and leaders to pay serious attention to their words.

- John Stuart Mill: "No great improvements in the lot of mankind are possible until a great change takes place in the fundamental constitution of their modes of thought."
- E. Paul Torrance: "The genius of the future will be the creative mind adapting itself to the shape of things to come. The skills of creative thinking must be recognized as mankind's most important adaptability skills. Such skills must become basic to the curriculum of schools, homes, business and other agencies."
- Jean Piaget: "The principal goal of education is to create men and women who are capable of doing new things, not simply of

repeating what other generations have done . . . men and women who are creative, inventive discoverers. The second goal of education is to form minds which can be critical, can verify and not accept everything they are offered."

- Luis Machado: "Everyone has, simply by existing, a right to be intelligent. And to be provided with a way to become consistently more intelligent. This is a right that must be recognized and held sacred. Above all, the necessary conditions for the exercise of this right must be available. This is society's mission and the primary obligation of its leaders. All of them."

CHAPTER 10

The Creative Business
of Educational Entrepreneurship

Of all the creatures of earth, only human baeings can change their patterns. Man alone is the architect of his destiny. Human beings, by changing the inner attitudes of their minds, can change the outer aspects of their lives.

— William James

Abstract: A review of trends in the specific teaching of thinking and problem-solving processes in higher education, with particular focus on arguments for the creation and introduction of courses in creative studies for graduate and undergraduate business programs as a fundamental profit-related business component. And the importance of "educational entrepreneurship" in initiating and promoting the development of a work force prepared for leadership in the dynamic, demanding, complex, global, interrelated world of business.

THE MESSAGE IS clear: Business, like the old grey mare, "ain't what she used to be." Few observers need to be reminded of the radical changes in the work place in response to new developments across society. The Information Age, with its dramatic developments in technology and communication systems, drives and demands constant change. The explosion of human affairs into a global, complex, interrelated system opens up new challenges and opportunities in the market place of new ideas. Workers at all levels lack many of the skills and talents required in the shifting complexities of modern business. Such a lack translates readily to lower productivity and limited profit.

Educational programs designed to prepare students to function effectively in the practical world of business traditionally focused on skills and practices of a more familiar system, leaving the business of thinking creatively and critically in many cases to chance. New ideas are often met with organized resistance. The world of work often seems to be "proud of machines that think, and suspicious of men and women who try to." Now business is calling for innovative, creative problem solvers. Risk takers and change makers are finding new encouragement. In enlightened business settings intrapreneurs are granted more freedom to think and to produce new ideas for the market place. Corporations report plans to increase the teaching of problem solving, creative thinking, teamwork, and other basic skills in training and development programs. Managers and administrators will not have to wait for on-the-job training and development in creative thinking and problem solving if educational entrepreneurs recognize and seize opportunities to provide leadership in the design and introduction of formal courses in thinking up, down, and sideways.

An awareness is growing in academic circles of the discipline of creativity as a component of educational psychology and a critical factor in human development. The Creative Education Foundation in Buffalo, New York, has been providing leadership in the understanding of the creative person, process, product, and press (environment) for nearly fifty years. It provides an international center for research and literature in creativity for individuals, organizations, and throughout the human experience.

As early as 1983 a survey across the entire population of U.S. colleges found that roughly 6% of those responding (1,188) offered formal courses in creativity. Minnesota reported three colleges with such a course. Indiana, Massachusetts, California, Michigan, Pennsylvania, and Virginia reported four or five. New York reported ten. Twenty-two other states reported one or two (McDonough, 1987). A similar survey today could result in a substantial increase in numbers.

As an example, an early report of the Minnesota colleges included St. Thomas, Augsburg College, and Metropolitan State University. In the case of St. Thomas, the complete report showed that formal courses in creative studies were taught in a number of departments and available to students across disciplines. An undergraduate course in entrepreneurial creative thinking and problem solving, required for the entre-preneurship minor and major, attracted students from a broad variety of other programs; a course on the creative process was offered in the masters in business communication program; a course in the discipline of creativity: Current Directions was a requirement in a Graduate Education Gifted/Creative/Talented Program, and available as an elective in other programs. The interdisciplinary nature of courses in creativity provides an obvious example of educational progress toward the ideal of teaching integrative, systemic processes of thought so critical in an increasingly complex, interactive world.

Why do most colleges and universities move so slowly in incorporating the teaching of creative thinking and problem solving processes into their official programs? Possible reasons were suggested by McDonough (1987) based on interviews with senior faculty members from a cross-section of college disciplines. It can be assumed that the same reasons continue to apply.

- Difficult challenge for traditional colleges to deviate from standard courses.
- Course in creativity requires the professor to surrender the position of authority to assist students in releasing their creative ability.
- Course in creativity requires the encouragement of a high level of student involvement, an attitude of flexibility, playfulness, and the enthusiastic commitment and belief in the concept that everyone possesses a creative ability. These requirements may not fit the style of some faculty members.
- Difficult to apply a letter grade to the student's knowledge of creativity.
- Generally, it is the faculty member who is enthusiastic about creativity and not the college administration who develops and promotes the course. That type of person may not be at each college.
- It is easier to simply continue to do what has been done in the past.

Other possible reasons include the exclusion of teachers of integrative studies in departments with a specific academic focus and the accompanying power of political influence on academic programming.

A growing interest in entrepreneurship, intrapreneurship, and small business development provides an alternative to a job within an established business or corporation. The loss of creative productive workers to independent business development led to the option of intrapreneurial roles for some workers within a company. Could it be that educational institutions are ready to recognize the role of educational entrepreneurs in the same way that the business community is encouraging risk takers and change makers?

Developing academic attention to the deliberate teaching, not only of creative thinking and problem solving, but to the full range of intellectual potential "way beyond the IQ," as suggested by Guilford (1977) is of growing importance in schooling at all levels. Recent new understandings of individual differences in learning and thinking styles offer critical clues to effective teaching. Formal courses in creative and critical thinking integrate well with related concepts of higher levels of thinking and behaving associated with ethics, thinking at a level of paradox, recognizing relationships, perceiving systems, and sensing future implications of recognizable trends in business, politics, and social issues.

Some years ago Peter Drucker, leading authority on management, advised educators in his article, "How Schools Must Change" (1989), "to start equipping students with the skills to work effectively in organizations, where most Americans now make their living." The trend in business, as well as in all of society's institutions, needs to be toward a reinterpretation of leadership that will be less stratified and "more egalitarian and dependent on individual responsibility, initiative and constant, open communication between individuals, regardless of organizational rank. . . . Direction and discipline will come from within, not from above, through interaction among 'colleagues' at all levels" (Drucker, 1989).

Margaret Wheatley (1992, 1996) promoted a similar movement toward a transformation of leadership to "self-organizing systems" in business and social institutions for the past decade. According to

Wheatley, "there is a simpler and more effective way to lead organizations that engages our desire to contribute, learn and find meaning in the world. We want organizations that can grow and change" (Wheatley, 1996).

> New understandings of human potential and the value of human differences in an interactive, integrated organizational operation are studied and discussed in business journals with increasing frequency. The call for creativity and innovation in bureaucracies is a call for serious reminders of the theoretical nature of investigations into human behavior. The study of human behavior underscores the good news that much of what is needed in times of intense change is available in the unlimited capacities of the human mind set free to think, to communicate new ideas, and to contribute. (Bleedorn, 1987)

Training and development programs in business are increasing their attention to seminars in creative thinking and problem-solving. That reality should motivate educational institutions to move with greater energy and urgency toward providing students with the understanding of their own creative potential and ways of stimulating and operationalizing their talents for innovation. The competitive global economy and profit motives demand such talents. When Paul Cook discusses "The Business of Innovation" (Taylor, 1990), he says, "To be an innovative company, you have to ask for innovation. It's that simple—and that hard." He might have added, "It's that real."

After mastery of the skills of business and technological performances, what remains to be added to the success formula is its most powerful, intricate, and diverse factor, the human asset. As evidence of the importance of the topic, in 1988 Harvard published a collection of articles, *People: Managing Your Most Important Asset.*

The potential for creative contributions to organizations of all kinds is unlimited. A major task is to remove the limitations imposed on the creative mind and spirit by society, education, the work environment, and the culture. The measurement, analyses, and compartmentalization of human traits, behaviors, and differences offer little real insight and application to the larger, systemic vision of fully functioning, creative, interactive minds working together to meet organizational goals. It is as someone once observed: we stand on the backs of whales to fish for minnows.

Both education and business sit on a threshold of new realities . One of the components of the paradigm shift is the activation of the unlimited thinking potential that is so available but often denied and unused. A major challenge faces both business and educational institutions: to free up human resources from the organizational constraints that prevent their full participation and contribution. The teaching of creative thinking, critical thinking, problem solving, and decision making is essential to prepare students for future business careers. Business schools need educational entrepreneurs who recognize the importance of formal courses and course components in thinking processes, and can establish a place for them in curricula.

The case for creative leadership can be taken to a level beyond business and organizations to address the emerging question of planetary survival.

> Therefore it is in the best interest of the species, from an evolutionary point of view, for individuals with problem-solving attributes, as well as those possessing other creative and innovative traits, to be recognized. This requires an attitude and a system directed to the selection of those who would also serve the species' interest and not only the interest of the individual. The present serious human predicament requires all our creative energies for its resolution. (Salk, 1983)

CHAPTER 11

Creative Leadership for Global Futures:
Notes for Educators

A leader is best when people barely know he exists.
Not so good when people obey and acclaim him.
Worse when they despise him.
But of a good leader who talks little,
When his work is done, his aim fulfilled,
They will say, "We did it ourselves."

— *Lao Tzu*

IS THE INSTITUTION of education aware of the influence it is having on the development of leadership for a vastly different kind of world?

The work of James MacGregor Burns (1978) makes the distinction between transactional leadership and transforming leadership. He described transactional leadership as a process of "exchange of one thing for another" between leaders and followers. As a system, it reflects a familiar hierarchical pattern of bureaucratic management and levels of authority or control. In contrast, transforming leadership can "satisfy higher needs and engage the full person of the follower." His observations on the new levels of mutuality possible between leaders and followers significantly redefined integrative "leadership" as a more effective alternative to hierarchical "management."

⑥

Research on Leadership

The motivation for the study on leadership was based on the conviction that a survey of a cross-section of the population could provide the start of a better understanding of thinking talents for educators to cultivate and nourish in students and in themselves in preparation for the emerging global future. The study was conducted in the following way (Bleedorn, 1988).

In a modified application of the Delphi system for collecting considered opinions regarding a futuristic issue, an initial survey was made with a group of educationists at a national conference of the Education Division of the World Future Society. An open-ended question asking for perceptions of talents critical for effective leadership in the advancing global age resulted in a long list, which was compressed into a more workable list of 33 talents. That listing became the basis of the survey instrument for two additional groups of subjects: college students and business leaders. The three groups were asked to prioritize the listed talents according to personal perception of importance to leadership for global futures. In addition, participants were asked to indicate their perception as to which of the talents were being addressed currently in educational practices and which were not being addressed.

The data were tabulated and analyzed to determine results for each of the three separate populations of subjects and for the composite group of 105 subjects. Certain of the findings are of particular relevance to proponents of creativity.

1. Creativity scored highest by the composite group as critical for effective leadership in the global future. Second highest rating was assigned to change agent qualities. Academic skills scored third.
2. Qualities specifically associated with the discipline of creativity (flexibility, tolerance for ambiguity, risk taking, curiosity, and humor) were ranked at levels in a range from tenth to thirtieth by the composite group.
3. Composite responses to the survey question, "Which of the talents do you perceive to be addressed in current educational practices?" showed the following to be those most attended to, listed in a descending order: goal-directed talents, academic skills, organizational skills, communication skills, and information retrieval. The five talents perceived to be least addressed were visionary thinking, spirituality, ambiguity (tolerance for) synthesizing talents, and empathy (Bleedorn, 1988).

No correlation was evident between perceived talents for leadership and the degree to which those talents were being addressed in schools (see figure 11.1). Implications for educators concerned with improving the quality of teaching and learning are unmistakable. Issues of school management, teacher preparation, student-centered curricula, and visionary planning related directly to the message of the research results.

FIGURE 11.1 • Composite Group Perceptions: Contrasts Between Priority Talents for Global Leadership and Educational Attention to Each Talent

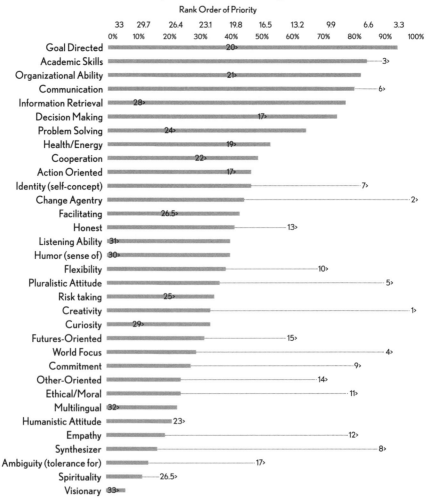

Percent of Population That Talent Is Being Addressed

ⓖ
What to Teach

Few would argue that, along with influences of family, genetics, economic status, and society in general, the mandated time spent in school significantly influences the thinking and attitudes of students as future citizens. Basic skills and knowledge traditionally took priority in school programs. Present federal requirements for assessment of learning through annual standardized tests do little to recognize many of the qualities perceived to be critical talents for leadership in a global future. Unless creativity, empathy, flexibility, vision, global awareness, tolerance for ambiguity, and ethical standards are taught and modeled by individual teachers, the application of skills and knowledge may be insufficient for positive human future development, both individually and collectively, even though standardized test scores may be high.

If the total focus in school programs is on standardized achievement as measured quantitatively, the qualitative factors of human development as suggested by the results of the leadership study will be left to chance. Numerous examples tell of smart citizens whose intellect fails the test of good, responsible citizenship. The need for educational leadership to acknowledge the importance of deliberately teaching processes of thinking is serious. It needs to be included in the official curricula at all levels of learning; and teacher candidates need to be screened for aptitude and attitude supportive of creative and other complex thinking processes.

ⓖ
Factor of Diversity

In a dynamic and interactive global society it is imperative that the world make the best possible use of the diversity of thinking talents. The natural resources of the world (productive land, clean water, oil, and minerals) may be finite, but the human mind possesses unlimited possibility for development (Bleedorn, 1998). It is incumbent on education to design into the 12 required years spent in school the maximum potential for growth and development of every student. It is the challenge of higher education to continue and expand the effort.

Harlan Cleveland, long-time international authority on leadership, refers to the role of education in world leadership.

> People are forever saying that leadership is an art, not a science or technology—a matter of instinct, not the product of thinking. The classroom is indeed an unlikely place to learn charisma. But leadership is the art that determines the social fallout of science and points technology toward human purposes. To relate them to each other is not carried in our genes. It has to be learned. So we educators cannot cop out; equipping minds for leadership ought to be what's "higher" about higher education. (1980)

Practical recommendations for the reform of higher education that appeared recently urged colleges and universities to "plan and implement a systemswide program for internationalizing the curriculum, not only from the perspective of specific international programs, but throughout the entire university" (Mestenhauser & Ellingboe, 1998).

Given the natural diversity of special interests and aptitudes among student populations, the need for flexibility and variety in academic programs is self-evident. It is reasonable to believe that all humans have an inherent urge to learn and grow, to enhance themselves, and to be recognized as significant in some way. The process of delivering learning is complicated by the fact that humans differ in their basic learning and thinking styles. Assessing achievement only on the basis of standardized tests is a serious limitation to the evaluation of student learning.

A positive self-concept depends upon the opportunity to think and be heard and to be publicly identified with a skill or talent of value to the community. Countless students at all levels of education show a change in their attitude, from apathetic to involved, when they learn to trust the teacher's invitation to express their creative ideas and when a classroom climate guarantees respect for diversity from their peers. The relationship among self-concept, antisocial behavior, and criminality has been the subject of study and speculation for a long time. Those who are denied the privilege of expression can be expected to express themselves in a drive for power and identity, often in a negative way. The positive contribution of every citizen according to his or her ability is what makes democracy work. Jefferson knew it and gave the nation good advice from the very beginning. Master teachers follow his advice and apply it to their work.

⑥

Global Futures

Changes in technology push humankind to new dimensions in their perceptions of reality. Pictures of the earth from space are scattered throughout our consciousness. Earth no longer has frames or boundaries, but is a global commons. It doesn't require much re-flection to realize that technology and communication systems inter-connect the global family socially, environmentally, economically, technologically and certainly politically. A less obvious, but equally dramatic development is the paradigm shift in the talents seen as important for effective leadership in a rapidly evolving "spaceship earth." If the goal of education is to prepare citizens to function in society, then it is time to view societies as extending beyond narrowly perceived nationalistic borders or systems. The Information Age with its electronic communication and information retrieval systems presents the potential to provoke not only better learning but also sthe understanding of differences and commonalities among people of planet Earth.

The computer age with its easy access to information and training delivers much of the learning traditionally taught within the institution of education. The missing ingredient in distance learning is the process of socialization. Human interaction and the stimulation of discourse that take place in a learning community are lost in the process of isolated, independent learning. Schools find themselves in the enviable position of being able to both develop quality thinking and learning and support the learner in the independent quest for growth and a positive identity with a sense of personal significance that turns that person toward service.

The current clamor for change in education throughout political and public settings cannot be ignored. Issues of dropout and underachievement, academic cheating, and the "dumbing down" of standards intensify the demand for attention. The recent publication, *The Cultural Creatives: How 50 Million People Are Changing the World*, reports that large numbers of people and groups "care deeply about ecology and saving the planet, about relationships, peace, and social justice, about self-actualization, spirituality, and self-expression" (Ray & Anderson, 2000). It was a surprise to discover that no reference to education was found in the index. Is it possible that education is perceived by society as being separate and unapproachable, having no relationship with problems and challenges of the times?

@

Summary

A most logical and rational conclusion is that education does indeed influence almost everything that happens in a democratic society. We are told that every important thing we do depends upon our habits of thought. School is about thinking, which makes the connection irrefutable. An irrevocably interconnected and complex global commons obligates us to educate for creative and other higher-order thinking processes and to cultivate in students an awareness of their potential for a life of personal growth and a productive role within the total system of society.

The teaching of creative thinking leads the way for the teaching of other complex thinking in a variety of content areas (Guilford, 1977). Specific attention to the broad array of human thinking processes highlights the need for more student-centered educational programs. It is not a new idea. As early as 1954, Alice Bailey was sharing this same message:

The true education is consequently the science of linking up the integral parts of man, and also of linking him up in turn with his immediate environment, and then with the greater whole in which he has to play his part. (Bailey, 1954)

Jerome Bruner (1963), outstanding authority in cognitive studies, believed more than 40 years ago that education was in a state of crisis, and was unresponsive to changing social needs. It lagged behind rather than led.

The current zeitgeist recognizes the need for radical changes in the nature of society and its global dimensions. The influence of educational experiences on human thought and behavior previously attracted little public attention. Mestenhauser and Ellingboe address the problem in their recent publication, *Reforming the Higher Education Curriculum: Internationalizing the Campus* (1998). Evidence suggests that the global mind was traditionally conditioned to focus and specialize rather than to comprehend the reality of the dynamic, systemic nature of all of life and the thinking patterns necessary to comprehend the entire dimensionality and function of human affairs. To quote John Stuart Mill, "No great improvements in the lot of mankind are possible until a great change takes place in the fundamental constitution of their modes of thought."

CHAPTER 12

You, There—What Do You Think?

*The teacher must not be perceived as pouring his knowledge
into the learner as though particles of the same knowledge
could pass from one subject to another.*

—*St. Thomas Aquinas*

WITH THE GROWING problem of school dropouts and disenchantment with learning comes an insistent call for change in schooling at all levels. This collection of ideas is designed to reaffirm the notion that students' minds can be engaged by giving them an opportunity to think and be heard without fear of rejection.

The most valuable resource in a changing world is the capacity of the people to think. The electronic age provides tools and services of astonishing strategic value, but it is the human brain/mind that provides the final humanity and the collective wisdom. Every participant in the world scene contributes to the creation of a just society. The 12 to 16 years of schooling available (mandated) for most citizens can help to develop and practice habits of thought that enhance the quality of individual life and the world community. Many observers of society believe that education's responsibility is to prepare the student mind/brain not only for learning, remembering, and arriving at an answer that fills the blank correctly, but also for thinking at complex levels where the answer is not predetermined.

⑥

The Right to Think

All humans are programmed for growth, for the enhancement of their knowledge, and ultimately for some significant place in the world. An early research study on human values showed that humans of all cultures, ages, genders, and economic levels share a basic value system (Arnspiger & Rucker, 1969). According to that study, all humans value affection, respect, skill, understanding, power and influence, goods and services, well-being, and responsibility.

Each day that a student spends at school in the company of and subject to the judgment of an authority and peers can add to or subtract from the values that affect individual attitude and sense of personal significance. The school day can be positive (an enhancement) or negative (a deprivation) of basic human values. The appearance of "responsibility" in the listing of shared human values has particular significance for creative teaching.

Implicit in the values is the opportunity within the school day to think according to the individual student level of intellect and to have one's ideas heard and respected. Opportunities for independent thinking can be provided without sacrificing the basic program. The fact is that teaching and learning are both enhanced when brief creative thinking exercises are provided at strategic intervals. They can be related to the specifics of the curriculum or they can be introduced as a mental break from memory or right-answer lessons.

Quality thinking exercises can be based on any of a number of thinking processes: creative, critical, problem-solving, evaluative, global, paradoxical, relational, systemic, futuristic transformational, or whatever else stimulates the mind to make new connections with what is already known or personally experienced. Directions for an exercise are most effective when they are clear, precise and open-ended with no predetermined right or best answer.

The following two examples demonstrate the importance of discovering individual thinking talents by offering a great variety of opportunities for recognizing special gifts of the mind.

A middle school student who had been identified as an at-risk student was withdrawn and downcast during a group discussion with a university student mentor. After some time he confided to the university student that "My teacher thinks I'm dumb." The teacher was missing the fact that the student was winning all the chess tournaments at the school. The student was struggling with the cognitive dissonance of polarized realities. The teacher was missing an important clue to a smart systemic thinker.

Another relevant experience comes from a long-term substitute teacher in a sixth-grade class who heard many warnings from other teachers and the principal that she would have to put up with Billy, who had an all-school reputation for being the most problematic student in the school's history. The way he stomped into the room confirmed the basis for the warnings. He was a problem. When the teacher talked with Billy's mother during a parental visit (his father had stopped coming because of the embarrassment), the teacher found some positive things to say about Billy and his energy, his leadership on the playground, his spirit. The mother was surprised to hear something besides negative reports and said, "Wait until I tell his father that you can even stand him." The breakthrough came later in the year when a visiting art instructor taught a paper-sculpture project and Billy made a large, quite convincing dragon in spite of the cutting and pasting overwhelming irregularities. The idea was remarkable and original enough, so the teacher displayed it along with some other examples of originality. The next day when Billy noticed his dragon in a place of honor, he turned around to the class and announced in a loud, triumphant voice, "Hey, she put mine up." He was a changed and cooperative student from that day and finished the school year with a dramatic record of achievement including the highest grade in the math final.

The following random list of ideas is for teachers who are looking for a few simple guidelines that can be used "as is" or adapted to some special content area. Most of the ideas will not need more than about five or ten minutes of class time. All of them have been used with effectiveness in student populations across a broad span of ages and backgrounds. All of them provide students with a reminder that:

- Sometimes school is for thinking "outside of the box," being seriously playful and playfully serious.
- The new mental connections of creative minds will be heard and respected by teachers and peers.

This list of general hints for teaching generally evokes response and involvement from students and persuades every student of his or her personal significance as an independent thinker.

◎

What Teaching Taught Me about Teaching

- It is inherent in all students to want to learn and grow and enhance themselves.
- Practically every student has something he or she loves to do and does well.
- It is important to design learning activities that represent a great variety of thinking skills and interests
- Sometimes it takes a long time to find the student's niche. Patience is required.
- Because the school day contains enough of memory, cognition, and convergent (right answer) thinking, try to present thinking activities that engage the mind in divergent (creative) thinking, evaluative (critical) thinking, systemic thinking, futuristic visionary thinking, transformational (producing change) thinking, paradoxical (entertaining two opposite truths) thinking, and most of all, keep it all on the light side.
- Remembering a student's name is less important than recognizing something special about every one. Students are neither a name nor a category nor a number nor a research statistic. At any age they are highly complicated social, physical, intellectual interactive systems, and being so recognized is vital to their thinking, self-concept, and motivation.
- We live in an organic world. Technological communications via symbols need a generous addition of realistic personal human and real world, organic learning experiences.
- Acknowledge the importance of assessment, but join the teacher movement to provide relief from the drudgery of overemphasis on standardized testing, scoring, reporting that interferes with a teacher's freedom to teach and removes the normal excitement of learning

from the school program. An alternative to standardized testing has been recently introduced by Grant Wiggins (1998). His "Educative Assessment" design is based on the principle that assessment should be "deliberately designed to improve and educate student performance, not merely to audit it." His ideas are both provocative and helpful.

- Participate in efforts to bring administration, teachers, parents, and students together in preparing students to function in a dynamically changing complex world and work place.
- Visit the writing of E. Paul Torrance (1995), Torrance and Safter (1990), and J. P. Guilford (1977) for practical and theoretical fundamentals on education that go "Way Beyond the IQ" and remind us that along with a student-centered focus on "How smart are you?" there can be a focus on discovering "How are *you* smart?"

⑥
What Do You Think?

The following examples of short, thinking exercises can be used to introduce a lesson or unit or to provide a playful break (mental recess) at strategic times during the school day. The exercises reinforce the fact that school can be serious and playful at the same time. They discover and cultivate qualities of thought that set the mind free for the expression of original mental connections and contribute to a sense of identity and personal significance.

These startup ideas are listed randomly without designation for particular groups or ages, including adult learners. Teachers can experiment with the ideas "as is" or adapt them for specific application to course content.

Many creative teachers are already well rehearsed in the art of inventing their own breakaway thinking activities. This collection includes challenges that exercise a full range of quality thinking beyond memory and right-answer responses. They provide students with mental challenges that stretch their minds, activate their curiosities, and acquaint them with the diverse operations of their minds. They stimulate the intellectual potential and, like football practice before the big game, prepare the mental muscles of the mind for the serious game of life.

- A basic requirement for creative teaching is to teach/review the rules for brainstorming: Either individually or in small groups, free up the brain to produce quantities of ideas or alternatives for solving a problem; discipline the mind to allow absolutely no judgment of any kind; relax and engage/enjoy the fantasy mind; listen to the group for clues to additional ideas. These rules are part of the discipline of creativity and must be strictly enforced. At first, the unfamiliar freedom to produce creative connections may cause problems of order. Some students may need a bit of time to make the adjustment to "controlled freedom" of effective thinking, idea production, and problem-solving.
- The strict enforcement of the principle of deferred judgment during a brainstorming session can help to establish a general classroom climate for freedom to participate without threat of immediate attack on original ideas. Critical judgment or rank ordering of ideas comes *after* the idea production session.
- Be sure that students are familiar with the concept of right- and left-brain hemispheric differences (Orsnstein, 1996), and are acquainted with thinking patterns associated with each and the importance of balanced whole-brain thinking.
- Use terms from a lesson or use randomly chosen terms to create original metaphoric statements.

> Life is like . . .
> Peace is like . . .
> A hurricane is like . . .

Students may surprise you with the philosophical depth of their thinking.

- Speculate on possible imaginative futures. (Example: What would happen if the heads of government could regulate the weather?)

- Identify a current trend reported in the news and speculate where that trend will be next year? In five years? In fifty years?
- Make use of playful, brainstorming "warm-up" thinking tasks before beginning a serious class. Warm-ups can be designed to relate to the level of experience of students. (Examples: Why would anyone want to live on a farm? Make a list. Why would anyone not want to live on a farm? Make a list.)
- Design environmental brainstorm topics. (Examples: How to recycle old tires? plastic cups? etc.)
- In-five-minutes list. (Examples: Everything you can think of that is round; all the words you can think of that begin with the letter Q.)
- Practice thinking of forced relationships. (Examples: How are an iceberg and a new idea the same? How are a computer and a human brain different? The same?)
- Create a logo (symbol) for a business that provides environmental protection services (or any other business).
- Design a personal logo. Use symbols for what you believe or what you can do.
- Create a design for a dog-exercising machine (De Bono, 1970).
- Make a list of your various talents. What are you good at? Don't be shy.
- Make a list of everything that comes in threes. (Examples: red, white, and blue, or up, down, and sideways.)
- List all the ways you can think of to catch a rabbit. Use your imagination.
- List plus and minus features of riding a bus.
- How many different kinds of flavors do cooks use?
- Present a picture related to a lesson. What curiosities do you have about what is going on in the picture? List them. Studying the picture, what do you think will happen next?
- How is an owl like a scientist? Think of twenty different ways.
- Think of polarized concepts (Examples: light or dark, true or false, freedom or discipline.) Discuss the art of making unity of differences. Discuss meanings of paradoxical statements such as "We are all so much together that we are going to die of loneliness."

The list is endless. Creative teachers can invent thinking exercises related to the lesson or project that don't require much time and that can lift a spiritless class out of the doldrums if the climate for freedom of thought and mutual respect is maintained. Mental breaks for students can lighten the load for teachers as well as for students. Teachers with an aptitude for diversity and balance in their own thinking patterns find pleasure in exercising the art of teaching that engages students in a variety of levels of thought in a learning space of mutual trust and respect.

Epilogue

AT THIS TIME of serious concern for the preservation of our natural resources, attention must be paid to the preservation and development of the ultimate and limitless resource, the human brain. Enlightened educators the world over are beginning to recognize, cultivate, and reward student thinking that is complex, systemic, and futuristic—the level of thought that serves society in a new kind of complex, interrelated world.

Public attention to the need for new kinds of thinking in many of our institutions and throughout human affairs has escalated markedly even since the completion of the articles in this collection. The 10th International Conference on Thinking in England in June 2002 featured authorities on creativity, including Howard Gardner and Robert Sternberg. In addition to conference sessions on thinking, a variety of metacognitive perspectives from basic skills to philosophical thought and mindful management appeared on the program.

Current journal articles are discussing "Teaching Utopian Thinking," "The Rise of the Creative Class," problems of "endangered minds," "Inescapable Creativity," and a "groundswell of consciousness," to name a few.

Both leadership and followership require that the best possible use be made of the best possible thinking for a society in transition. The potential for complex, systemic, futuristic thought is present in most students. For some it is already there, waiting to be recognized. Almost every important thing we do depends on our habits of thought. Education can deliberately teach creative, integrative thinking at the same time that it teaches skills and facts. It may be that quality thinking should head the list of basic skills if we want to prepare students for a productive and meaningful life in a dynamically changing world and move that worlds into new patterns of environmental sustainability, trust and mutuality.

Reference List

Ackroyd, P. (1995). *Blake: A biography* New York: Alfred A. Knopf, Inc.

Amabile, T. M. (1983). *The social psychology of creativity.* New York: Springer Verlag.

Annan, K. (2002). Quoted in U.N. Association of Minnesota Brochure.

Arieti, S. (1976). *Creativity: The magic synthesis.* New York: Basic Books.

Arnspiger, V. C., Rucker, R., & Preas, M. E. (1969). *Personality in social process.* Dubuque, IA: Kendall/Hunt Publishing Company.

Bailey, A. (1954). *Education in the new age.* New York: Lucis Publishing Co.

Beuys, J. (1990). *Joseph Beuys in America: Writings by and interviews with the author.* Carin Kuoni (Ed.). New York: Four Walls Eight Windows.

Beuys, J.(1998). Creativity = Capital. Joseph Beuys Multiples Art Exhibition, Walker Art Center, Minneapolis.

Bleedorn, B. (1987, October–December). Creativity and innovation in bureaucracies: stimulating and facilitating creative ideas upward. *Value World,* 9–17.

Bleedorn, B. (1988). *Creative leadership for global futures: Studies and speculations.* New York: Peter Lang.

Bleedorn, B. (1989, May). The right to think. Paper presented at the International Conference on Building Understanding and Respect Between People of Diverse Religions or Beliefs, Warsaw, Poland.

Bleedorn, B. (1993). New think for the future: Educating the global brain. *Keystone: University of St. Thomas Minneapolis Campus Neighborhood Newsletter.*

Bleedorn, B. (1998). *The creativity force in education, business, and beyond: An urgent message.* Lakeville, MN: Galde Press.

Botkin, J., Elmandjra, M., & Malitza, M. (1979). *No limits to learning: Bridging the human gap.* New York: Pergamon Press.

Bruner, J. S. (1963). *The process of education: A searching discussion of school education opening new paths to learning and teaching.* New York: Vintage Books.

Burns, J. (1978). *Leadership*. New York: Harper and Row, 141–168.

Buzan, T., & Buzan, B. (1993). *The mind map book: How to use radiant thinking to maximize your brain's untapped potential*. New York: Penguin Books.

Capra, F. (1990, January–February). The crisis of perception, *The Futurist, 24*, 64.

Cleveland, H. (1980, August). Learning the art of leadership: The worldwide crisis in government demands new approaches, *Twin Cities Magazine*, 27–34.

Cleveland, H. (1984). Leaders as first birds off the telephone wire, *Leading Edge, 5*, 2.

Cleveland, H. (1985, July–August). Education for the information society. *Change*, 13–21.

Cleveland, H. (1985). *The knowledge executive: Leadership in an information society*. New York: E. P. Dutton.

Cleveland, H. (1986). Get-it-all-together. *Brain Mind Bulletin*, 4.

Cleveland, H. (1993). *Birth of a new world: An open moment for international leadership*. San Francisco: Jossey-Bass Publishers.

Cleveland, H. (1998). Endorsement, back cover of Bleedorn, *The creativity force in education, business, and beyond*.

Cleveland, H. (2001, July). The nobody-in-charge society: Chaotic or chaordic? Presentation at World Future Society Conference, Minneapolis.

Clinton, W. J. (2002, January 29). Transcript of a talk at the University of California, Berkeley.

Cousins, N. (1979). *The anatomy of an illness*. New York: W. W. Norton.

De Bono, E. (1970). *The dog exercising machine*. New York: Simon and Schuster.

De Bono, E. (1992). *Serious creativity: Using the power of lateral thinking to create new ideas*. New York: Harper Collins.

Drucker, P. (1989, May). How schools must change. *Psychology Today*.

Einstein, A. (1990). In Ed McGaa (Eagle Man), *Mother earth spirituality: Native American. paths to healing ourselves and the world*. San Francisco: Harper & Row, iii.

Etuk, E. (2002). *Great insights on human creativity: transforming the way we live, work, educate, lead and relate*. Blacksburg, VA, 95.

Fantini, M., & Weinstein, G. (1969). *Toward a contact curriculum*. New York: Anti-Defamation League of B'nai B'rith.

Florida, R. (2002, May). The rise of the creative class. *Washington Monthly*, 15–25.

Gardner, H. (1981, February). How the split brain gets the joke. *Psychology Today*, 74–78.

Gardner, H. (1985). *The mind's new science: A history of the cognitive revolution.* New York: Basic Books.

Gelb, M. (1998). *How to think like Leonardo da Vinci: Seven steps to genius every day.* New York: Delacorte Press.

Getzels, J. W., & Jackson, P. W. (1962). *Creativity and intelligence.* New York: Wiley.

Glaser, E. M. (1941). *An experiment in the development of critical thinking.* New York: AMS Press.

Gorbachev, M. (1988). *Perestroika: New ways of thinking for our country and the world.* New York: Harper and Row.

Gowan, J. (1968). *Creativity: Its educational implications.* New York: McGraw Hill.

Guilford, J. P. (1968). *Intelligence, creativity and their educational implications.* San Diego: Robert R. Knapp.

Guilford, J. P. (1977). *Way beyond the IQ: Guide to improving intelligence and creativity.* Buffalo, NY: Creative Education Foundation.

Harman, W., & Rheingold, H. (1984). *Higher creativity: Liberating the unconscious for breakthrough insights.* Los Angeles: Jeremy P. Tarcher, Inc.

Harman, W., & Hormann, J. (1990). *Creative work: The constructive role of business in a transforming society.* Indianapolis: Knowledge Systems, Inc.

Harvard College President and Fellows. (1988). People: Managing your most important asset.

Havener, C. (1999). *Meaning: The secret of being alive.* Edina, MN: Beaver's Pond Press, Inc.

Isaksen, S., & Murdock, M. (1988, March). The outlook for the study of creativity. An emerging discipline? Presented at the annual meeting of the American Association of Higher Education, Washington, DC.

Johnson, D., & Johnson, R. (1992). *Creative controversy.* Edina, MN: Interaction Book Company.

Koestler, A. (1964). *The act of creation.* New York: Dell Publishing Co.

Land, G., & Jarman, B. (1992). *Breakpoint and beyond: Mastering the future today.* New York: Harper Business.

Laszlo, E. (1992, September). The freedom of thought, expression and action in a just society. Presented at the Third International Dialogue on the Transition to a Global Society, Landegg Academy, Wienacht, Switzerland.

Laszlo, E. (2002, March–May). The quiet dawn. *IONS Noetic Sciences Review, 59,* 10.

Machado, L. (1983, July 18). The right to be intelligent. Reviewed in *Leading Edge,* 4.

MacKinnon, D. (1978). Reviewed in *In search of human effectiveness: Identifying and developing creativity.* Buffalo, NY: Bearly Limited, 186.

Maslow, A. (1973). *The further reaches of human nature.* New York: Viking Press.

Mayor, F. (1990, September). Global vision. Presented at the Third International Dialogue on the Transition to a Global Society, Landegg Academy, Wienacht, Switzerland.

McDonough, P., & McDonough, B. (1987). A survey of American colleges and universities on the conducting of formal courses in creativity. *The Journal of Creative Behavior, 21,* 271–282.

McGhee, P. (1979). *Humor: Its origin and development.* New York: W. W. Freeman.

Mestenhauser, J. (1997). The internationalization of higher education: A cognitive response to the challenges of the twenty-first century. Presented at the Ninth Annual Conference of the European Association for International Education, Barcelona, Spain.

Mestenhauser, J., & Ellingboe, B. (1998). *Reforming the higher education curriculum: Internationalizing the campus* Phoenix, AZ: Oryx Press.

Milbrath, L. (1996). *Learning to think environmentally while there is still time.* Albany, NY: State University of New York Press, 20.

Milbrath, L. (2001). Envisioning a sustainable environment. Chatauqua, NY: Chautauqua Institution (audio tape).

Millar, G. (1995). *E. Paul Torrance: "The creativity man."* Norwood, NJ: Ablex Publishing Corporation.

Ornstein, R. (1968). *The psychology of consciousness.* New York: Pelican Books.

Ornstein, R. (1996). *The mind field.* Cambridge, MA: A Malor Book ISHK.

Orr, D. (1994). *Earth in mind: On education, and the human prospect.* Washington, DC: Island Press.

Ouspensky, P. D. (1973). *The psychology of man's possible evolution.* New York: Vintage Books.

Parnes, S. (1981). *The magic of your mind.* Buffalo, NY: The Creative Education Foundation.

Paul, R. (1990). *What every person needs to survive in a rapidly changing world.* Santa Rosa, CA: Richard W. Paul Foundation for Critical Thinking.

Paul, R. (1993, September–October). The logic of creative and critical thinking. *American Behavioral Scientist, 37,* 21–39.

Piaget, J. (1950). *The psychology of intelligence.* London: Rutledge.

Prigogine, I. (1990, September). Global vision. Presented at the International Dialogue on the Transition to a Global Society, Landegg Academy, Wienacht, Switzerland.

Ray, P., & Anderson, S. R. (2000). *The cultural creatives: How 50 million people are changing the world.* New York: Harmony Books.

Renzuli, J. (2002). *Scales for rating the behavioral characteristics of superior students.* Revised edition. Manfield Center, CT: Creative Learning Press, Inc.

Ruggiero, V. (1988). *The art of thinking: A guide to critical and creative thought.*s New York: Harper & Row, frontispiece.

Russell, P. (1993). *The global brain.* Los Angeles: Jeremy P. Tarcher, Inc.

Salk, J. (1983). *Anatomy of reality: Merging institution and reason.* New York: Columbia University Press.

Shelldrake, R. (1983). *A new science of life.* Los Angeles: Jeremy P. Tarcher, Inc..

Stein, M. (Ed.) (2001). *Creativity's global correspondents—2001.* Delray Beach, FL: Winslow Press.

Sternberg, R. (1988). *The nature of creativity: Contemporary psychological perspectives.* Cambridge, MA: Cambridge University Press.

Taylor, W. (1990, March–April). The business of innovation: An interview with Paul Cook. *Harvard Business Review.*

Tobias, S. (1986, March–April). Peer perspectives on the teaching of science. *Change,* 36–41.

Torrance, E. P. (1962). *Guiding creative talent.* New York: Prentice Hall.

Torrance, E. P. (1979). *The search for satori and creativity* Buffalo, NY: Creative Education Foundation & Creative Synergetic Associates.

Torrance, E. P., & Safter, H. T. (1990). *The incubation model of teaching: Getting beyond the aha!.* Buffalo, NY: Bearly Limited.

Torrance, E. P. (1995). *Why fly? A philosophy of creativity.* Norwood, NJ: Ablex Publishing Corporation.

Torrance, E. P., & Safter, H. T. (1999). *Making the creative leap beyond.* Buffalo, NY: Creative Education Foundation Press.

Thant, U. (1963, June). Education in our changing times. Commencement Address at Mt. Holyoke College.

Webster. (1976). *International unabridged dictionary of the English language.* Springfield, MA: G. C. Merriam Co.

Wellstone, P. (2001). *The conscience of a liberal.* New York: Random House.

Wheatley, M. J. (1992). *Leadership and the new science: Learning about organization from an orderly universe.* San Francisco: Berrett-Koehler.

Wheatley, M. J. (2002). *Turning to one another: Simple conversations to restore hope.* San Francisco: Berrett-Koehler.

Wheatley, M. J., & Kellner-Rogers, M. (1996). *A simpler way.* San Francisco: Berrett-Koehler.

Wiggins, G. (1998). *Educative assessment: Designing assessments to inform and improve student performance.* San Francisco: Jossey-Bass, Inc.

Yau, C. (2002). *Breakthrough and Beyond: Twentieth Century Scientific Revolutions and Artistic Innovations.* St. Catherines, Ontario: Lincoln Graphics Press, 66–69.

Index

local changes in educational programming, 15
Locke, John, 28

M
Machado, Luis Alvaro, ix, 71
MacKinnon, D., 10, 42
Malitza, M., 3, 41, 65, 70
Maraviglia, Frank, 54
Maslow, A., 50
mathematics education, 15. *See also* basic
skills teaching
Mayor, Frederico, 1
McDonough, P. & B., 73, 74
McGhee, P., 51
"megatruth," 57
Mestenhauser, J., 59, 64, 82, 85
metaphors. *See* similes and metaphors
Metropolitan State University, 73
Milbrath, Lester, 18, 21, 37
Mill, John Stuart, 70, 85
Millar, G., 59
mind mapping, 23, 25
"morphic resonance" theory, 34
Murdock, M., 42

N
No Limits to Learning (Botkin,
Elmandjera, and Malitza), 41, 65

O
originality, 7, 30
Ornstein, R., 50, 91
Orr, David, 20, 21, 25
Osborn, Alex, 55
Ouspensky, P. D., 8–9

P
paradoxical thinking, 2, 13, 37, 38, 43,
67, 89
Parnes, S., 7, 44, 55
Paul, Richard, 44, 67
peace, xvi, 17
peace studies, 13
*People: Managing Your Most Important
Asset* (Harvard), 76
*Perestroika: New Thinking for Our Country
and the World* (Gorbachev), 45

"Persecution of Creativity," 56
Piaget, Jean, xviii, 12, 70
planetary survival. *See* environmental
issues
Plato, 6, 28
preference for complexity, 30
Prigogine, Ilya, 1
problem solving. *See* creative problem-
solving process
problem student, example of, 88
products of thought, 19–20
purpose of collected articles, xvii–xix

Q
qualitative education vs. standardization,
38, 81
quality thinking processes, xix, 36–37,
66–71; and educational reform,
67–68; group applications, 68–69;
and humor, 49; teaching of, xix, 87,
95

R
Ray, P., 23, 84
reading. *See* basic skills teaching
reality-based learning, 17
*Reforming the Higher Education Cur-
riculum: Internationalizing the Campus*
(Mestenhauser & Ellingboe), 85
Renzulli, J., 47
research on leadership, 78–80
"Resurrection of Creativity," 56
right-brain thinking, 23, 28, 50, 91
right to thought. *See* Freedom of thought
Risk taking, 8, 30, 39, 73, 79
Rucker, R., 87
Ruggiero, Vincent Ryan, 41, 63
Russell, Peter, 34

S
Safter, H. T., 24, 62, 90
St. Thomas, 73–74
Salk, Jonas, 46, 77
satire, 51
science education, 15, 16
self-actualization, 50
self-concept, 82, 83
sensitivity, 30

Shapiro, Robert B., vii
Sheldrake, Rupert, 34
similes and metaphors, 91; comic simile, 51
simultaneous thinking, 50
Skromme, Arnold, xiv
small business development and entrepreneurship as course of study, 74, 75
Socrates, 6
standardized testing, 24, 38, 68, 81, 82, 89–90
Stein, Morris, 9, 36
Sternberg, R., 42, 94
superconscious mind, 57
synectics, 31
systemic thinking, 13, 18, 23, 24, 37, 67, 88, 89

T
Taylor, W., 76
teacher education, xix, 61, 64, 81
teachers: as agents for educational reform, 61; benefits of creative teaching principles and strategies, 38; conventionally conditioned, 15; and educational reform, 14, 68; ideas about teaching and classroom exercises, 24–25, 88–93; need for recruiting more, 60, 61–62
technology and learning, 37, 68, 70, 89. *See also* information era
testing. *See* standardized testing
Thant, U, 3, 32
thinking diversity. *See* diversity
thinking processes, xv; divergent and convergent, 44; importance of, 14, 40, 44; for a just society, 2–4; recognition and development of, xix; teaching of, 4–5, 13, 14, 24, 39
Thoreau, Henry David, 18
Tobias, Sheila, 15
tolerance for ambiguity, 8, 30, 79, 81

Torrance, E. Paul: as authority on creativity, xiii–xiv, xvii, 4–5, 17, 59; on design of creative thinking activities, 24, 62, 70, 90; "Incubation Model of Teaching" originated by, 13, 62; recognizing cognitive factors of creativity, 30; on sense of humor, 47; studies of creativity by, 42
Torrance Tests of Creative Thinking, 6, 62
transactional leadership, 33, 78
transformations, 19–20, 56, 67, 89
transforming leadership, 33, 45, 57, 78
trust, 39, 64
truth, 43

U
United Nations Chapter, xvi
United Nations' Universal Declaration of Human Rights, 43
Units, classes, and relationships, at low end of Guilford hierarchy, 7, 19, 23, 58, 67
unity, 6
universal education, 9–10
universities. *See* higher education
university of St. Thomas, 73–74

V
visionary thinking. *See* futuristic thinking

W
Weinstein, G., 22
Wellstone, Paul, 38
Wheatley, Margaret, 75–76
"whole brain" thinking, 15, 91
Wiggins, G., 38, 90
wisdom, 64
witticism, 51
work force: changing nature of, vi–vii; skills needed, 72. *See also* business
World Future Society, xvi, 8, 39, 67, 79
World Peace Movement, xvi

About the Author

BERENICE BLEEDORN IS an educational entrepreneur, and has initiated and taught courses in creative studies and futures studies for more than 30 years in both education and business departments of various universities. She has provided seminars and workshops locally, nationally, and internationally, with a focus on the academic and practical nature of the discipline of creativity and other higher-order thinking processes. She was a faculty member of the University of St. Thomas for 17 years, where she founded the Institute for Creative Studies.

Dr. Bleedorn has been a colleague of the Creative Education Foundation in Buffalo, New York, for 35 years and has been honored with both their Service Commitment and Distinguished Leader awards. She is a member of the lieutenant governor's advisory committee on education in Minnesota and is the author of *The Creativity Force in Education, Business, and Beyond: An Urgent Message*. Her B.S. in education and M.A. in educational psychology are from the University of Minnesota. Her doctorate in leadership and human behavior is from United States International University in San Diego.